THE WAY *of* JUDO

THE WAY
of JUDO

◉

*A Portrait of Jigoro Kano
and His Students*

JOHN STEVENS

SHAMBHALA
Boulder
2013

SHAMBHALA PUBLICATIONS, INC.
2129 13th Street
Boulder, Colorado 80302
www.shambhala.com

9 8 7 6 5

Printed in the United States of America

Shambhala Publications makes every effort to print on acid-free,
recycled paper.

Shambhala Publications is distributed worldwide by
Penguin Random House, Inc., and its subsidiaries.

LIBRARY OF CONGRESS CATALOGING-IN-PUBLICATION DATA

Stevens, John, 1947–
The way of judo: a portrait of Jigoro Kano
and his students / John Stevens.
p. cm.
ISBN 978-1-59030-916-2 (pbk.: alk. paper)
1. Kano, Jigoro, 1860-1938. 2. Martial artists—Japan—Biography.
3. Educators—Japan—Biography. 4. Judo—History. I. Title.
GV1113.K36S84 2013
796.8092—DC23
[B]
2012044707

Contents

v

Preface

Jigoro Kano was a seminal figure in the modernization of Japan who also played an important role on the world stage. He was the founder of Kodokan judo, the most important educator in the country, a member of the Diet, the father of physical education in Japan, and an international spokesman for both the Japanese Olympic Committee and the nation itself. This is his story, public and private, along with profiles of the main teachers and colleagues who influenced Kano throughout his life. Since Kano's interaction with his disciples is an integral part of his saga, this portrait includes an extensive chapter on the lives of his principal students, East and West.

The translations from Japanese to English are by the author. Japanese names are in Western style, family name last. All the relevant resource and reference material is given in detail in the back matter "Resources" section.

John Stevens
Honolulu, 2013

THE WAY *of* JUDO

1

The Public Career
of Jigoro Kano

●

SHUT OFF FROM THE WORLD for more than two centuries by the
Tokugawa shoguns, Japan ended its long isolation on March 31,
1854, with the signing of the Treaty of Kanagawa. The old order
in Japan quickly crumbled as the island nation prepared to meet
the world. It was a period of stupendous change and immense
challenge; the entire social, political, and economic landscape
of Japan would be transformed within a few decades. Just as this
new era was dawning in Japan, Jigoro Kano was born, on October
28, 1860, in Mikage.

Overlooking placid Osaka Bay and backed by the majestic
Rokko mountain range, Mikage (now part of Kobe City) was
then one of the most pleasant areas of western Japan. The re-
gion is blessed with a temperate climate, tasty rice, and pure
water, three natural resources put to good use in sake brewing, still one of the primary industries of the district. For more
than three centuries, the Kano family was a main sake-brewing
clan (they produced the highly popular Kiku-Masamune brand,
among others). In fact, the name *Kano* means "production of delightful sake."

Kano's father's original name was Mareshiba Shogenji (1813–
85). The Shogenji family served as the hereditary keepers of the
Hie Shrine in Omi. Mareshiba chose to become a Confucian
scholar rather than a Shinto priest. He was hired as a home tutor
in the Chinese classics for the Kano children. Mareshiba ended up

marrying Sadako, one of the daughters, and then being adopted into the Kano family, thereafter assuming the name Jirosaku.

Five children were born to Jirosaku and Sadako, three boys and two girls. Kano was the last child. His birth name was Shinnosuke. Later, he was called Jigoro ("fifth child of Jiro"). The Kano family was wealthy so the children grew up in a home—named "Pavilion of a Thousand Sails" because so many boats passed by on the placid nearby bay—that was among the largest and best appointed in the area. The Kano family property stretched to the seashore so Kano spent much of his childhood outdoors playing on the beach and swimming in the ocean.

While Kano's early circumstances were enviable, his upbringing was strict and disciplined in traditional samurai style. Kano had fond memories of a kind and considerate mother, but he also remembered her as someone who would not tolerate any kind of improper behavior and counseled him to always be considerate to others. For example, neighborhood children would gather to play in the Kano's family's large garden. When his mother made treats for the children, she had them stand in line with Kano at the end. Sometimes there were no more treats left when it was his turn. "They are your guests," his mother told him. "Others first." Jirosaku made sure that his son received the best education, arranging for special tutoring by Chiku'un Yamamoto (1819–88), an eminent Confucian scholar, calligrapher, painter, seal carver, and tea master. Young Kano studied with Yamamoto from age seven to eleven. Even as a child, Kano himself was a teacher. From the time he was eight years old, Kano began giving his relatives' kids lessons in what he had learned from Yamamoto.

Following his wife Sadako's death in 1869—Jigoro was nine years old at the time—Jirosaku moved the family to Tokyo. Jirosaku was never interested in sake brewing; he was more involved with shipping it together with other cargo. Jirosaku became an entrepreneur in the shipping industry—he was one of the original members of Japan's first international trading company—and also served as a high-ranking government official in the maritime agency. As he was growing up, Kano remembers his father as mostly absent. In Tokyo, Kano moved to a boardinghouse when he was thirteen years old and saw his father even less. (Jirosaku died in 1885 after a long and successful private and public career. Kano stayed in touch with his father over the years, but they did not seem to be especially close. However, that was the norm for relationships between father and son in those days.)

Early Education

In 1870, at age ten, Kano enrolled in the Seitatsu Shojuku, a private academy operated by the scholar Keido Ubukata. Ubukata's father, Teisai (1799–1856), was a famous Edo period swordsman and calligrapher, but a very bad drunk. After a drunken rage at a restaurant, Teisai was followed home by a group of swordsmen who cut him down at the gate of his academy. The assassins were disciples of the swordsman Keishiro Kenko (1814–64). Kenko was expelled from his domain after the incident, but the actual assassin is unknown. Keido, who was ten years old at the time, swore to avenge his father. Keido pursued his vendetta for twenty years, but it was never settled. Keido was unable to discover who the actual killer of his father was, plus the new Meiji government prohibited the carrying out of vendettas. Keido was thus compelled to focus his energy on a different method of honoring his father, himself becoming a top calligrapher and teacher.

Keido became head of the Seitatsu Shokuju Academy founded by his father. The academy was unique for that time in that it accepted not only the offspring of aristocrats and high-ranking samurai (heretofore learning was exclusively a privilege of the upper classes) but also children of merchants, craftsmen, restaurateurs, and others, some of whom were in training, among other things, to be sumo wrestlers, kabuki actors, and geisha. Keido became a highly regarded calligrapher in the tradition of his father as well as a scholar. In addition to drilling his pupils in the classics of China and Japan, he made each student submit, daily, three notebooks full of sample brushwork. In the evening after classes,

Keido often held informal discussions on contemporary affairs, and he told Kano that while a classical education was invaluable, from now on Japanese students needed to acquaint themselves thoroughly with Western culture and learning.

Taking Keido's advice to heart, Kano initially studied English at the Sanki Academy of Shubei Mitsukuri, and then, in 1873, he entered the Ikuei Gijuku, a more advanced academy where all the courses were taught in English or German by foreign instructors (the mathematics textbook was in Dutch). In the dormitory, the brilliant, well-bred, and somewhat snobbish Kano was subject to severe hazing by jealous seniors, against whom he found himself defenseless. Kano rued this sorry state of affairs, and it was during this troublesome period that he first heard of jujutsu, a martial art that was supposed to enable a soft physical force to control a hard attack. Kano was not able to practice until later, but he did try to build up his body by engaging in various sports, including the newly introduced game of baseball. Kano was a pitcher.

In 1874, Kano entered the Tokyo School of Foreign Languages, where he had to learn English all over again. His previous English teachers had been Dutch or German, and when faced with British and American native pronunciation, he was at a total loss as to what was being said. Kano's assiduous study of English under difficult conditions was remarkable. Dictionaries were scarce in those days, so the students at the academy were obliged to share the single textbook available. Prior to exams, Kano's "textbook shift" was from 1:00 A.M. to 5:00 A.M. Despite such obstacles, Kano mastered the language, keeping a diary in English most of his adult life. (Later Kano was to write his *bujutsu* [martial art] technical notes in English as well, probably to keep them secret). After graduating from the language school, Kano entered the Kaiseki Academy, another government-sponsored school. In 1877, the academy became Tokyo University, and Kano had the distinction of being a student of the nation's premier educational institution. The first freshman class had eight students; Kano's freshman class the following year had six. In 1878, Kano also began to take night classes at Nissho Gakusha, an institution of higher learning that focused on Chinese literature.

Kano was always a rational thinker and liked the precision of mathematics and science. He was also interested in astronomy. He thought he would major in science but decided to switch to the humanities instead, feeling that the humanities (history, economics, political science, aesthetics, and ethics) would give him a broader view of human nature, and how society functioned. Throughout his life, Kano wanted education to make him a better, not just a smarter, person.

In many ways, the education that Kano received at Tokyo University was ideal. The facility was divided between Japanese and Western professors. (Actually, there were more Western professors, twenty-seven to twelve.) The Western professors lectured on such subjects as English literature, world history, economics, ethics, aesthetics, Western philosophy, the social and natural sciences, and the like, while the Japanese professors taught the classics of Chinese and Japanese literature, Asian history, and philosophy. Kano's English professor was an American, William Houghton (1852–1917).

Ernest Fenollosa (1853–1908) was the professor who had the greatest lasting influence on Kano. Fenollosa had come from Salem, Massachusetts, to Japan in 1878 to teach philosophy and economics at the university. Fenollosa introduced Kano to the ideas of the British philosopher Herbert Spenser (1820–1903), particularly Spenser's book *The Theory of Education*. Spenser described a perfect education as one that educated the mind, morals, and body of a human being. Spenser argued that it was possible for a perfect society to evolve if human beings perfected their characters through proper intellectual, moral, and physical education. Under Fenollosa's four-year tutelage, Kano learned about modern Western educational philosophy and later how important it is to appreciate the beauty and significance of Asian culture. Thanks to Fenollosa's influence, Kano later aspired to make Kodokan judo be both an education of the body and mind as well as an aesthetic pursuit.

Another favorite professor of Kano's was the eccentric Zen

priest Tanzan Hara (1819–1892), who taught Indian philosophy. Hara had little use for the trappings of religion, a view Kano shared wholeheartedly. Hara has been immortalized in modern Zen lore as the hero of the following oft-repeated tale:

Two novice monks, Tanzan and Ekido, were on a pilgrimage from one training monastery to another. A storm blew up, and the pair came to a flooded crossroad that had been transformed into a fast-flowing stream. A lovely young girl was stranded there. Tanzan inquired, "Do you need help?" When the girl replied, "Yes," he lifted her up on his shoulders, carried her across the flooded road, and deposited her safely on the other side. After the two monks walked a bit farther, Ekido burst out, "How could you do such a thing? You know it is strictly prohibited for Buddhist monks to touch women!" (And on top of that, in those days, Japanese women did not use underwear.) Tanzan shot back, "What? Are you still carrying that girl? I put her down long ago."

Hara went on to become dean of Komazawa University and was later elected to the Japan Academy. In 1892, the seventy-three-year-old Hara sat in Zazen and asked for a stack of postcards to be addressed to his followers and friends. He wrote on each one, "Please be advised that I am going to die now. Goodbye." After he finished the stack, he closed his eyes and died in the meditation posture.

Kano's Physical Training

Kano graduated from Tokyo University in 1881 and stayed on for another year of graduate study of philosophy and economics. The two pillars of Kano's lifelong scholarship were the Chinese and Japanese classics and English literature, a blend of Eastern and Western wisdom, traditional philosophy and modern thinking.

During this period of academic success, however, Kano once again found himself confronted by bullies and ruffians both on and off campus, and he became more determined than ever to learn jujutsu. At that particular moment in Japanese history, it was not easy to find a suitable teacher.

During the Tokugawa period (1860–1868), each domain in Japan employed martial arts instructors as a matter of course—the Date domain in northern Japan at one time had more than two hundred instructors teaching every kind of martial art imaginable—and nearly every samurai man and woman received extensive training in bujutsu. However, once the feudal system collapsed in 1868, domain support for martial arts academies ceased, and almost all dojos were forced to close. Furthermore, with the increasing modernization of the country, most Japanese lost interest in the classical martial arts. "Times have changed, and such things are neither useful nor relevant," Kano was bluntly admonished not only by his father but even by many former martial artists.

Nevertheless, Kano persisted for nearly two years. Since he knew that many martial artists had become bonesetters to make a living, he stopped by clinic after clinic. Finally, at the clinic of Teinosuke Yagi, he met someone who could help him find a jujutsu instructor. Yagi was not teaching jujutsu anymore himself, but he introduced Kano to Hachinosuke Fukuda (1828–79), of the Tenjin Shin'yo ryu. This ryu (martial art system), established by Mataemon Iso (d. 1862), was a comparatively new style of jujutsu, emphasizing *atemi* (strikes to anatomical weak points) and grappling techniques. It is said that Mataemon developed many of his tactics in the street, fighting groups of rogues that terrorized the populace (law and order had largely broken down near the end of the shogunate). He supposedly knew an impressive 124 types of punches. He needed to: he fought a number of battles against group attacks, and thus had to master the ability to down each attacker with a single blow delivered at tremendous speed in order to avoid being overwhelmed. In all, there were 240 basic techniques in the Tenjin Shin'yo ryu syllabus. At one time, Iso was said to have had five thousand students. That was in the old days.

One of Mataemon's top disciples, the formidable Hachinosuke Fukuda—a former instructor of jujutsu at the Kobusho (national martial arts academy)—now made a living as a bonesetter. (The Tenjin Shin'yo ryu had been noted for the high quality of its bonesetting skills.) He had a small dojo with five students. In 1877, at

A photo of the intent, determined young Kano, full of dynamic energy. This was likely taken not long after he began practicing jujutsu.

the age of seventeen, Kano was accepted by Fukuda as a trainee. Kano threw himself wholeheartedly into the training, expecting and getting no quarter; if no one else showed up—Fukuda was in fact rather ill, frequently confined to bed—Kano practiced alone, executing various movements with a heavy iron rod Fukuda had given him. Training was tough, in the old style, with plenty of punches, kicks, throws, pins, and chokes. Kano covered his aching body with a potent but foul-smelling salve of his own concoction and thus quickly became known among his classmates as "Kano the Odiferous." Every night, upon returning home, he would carefully demonstrate for his brother and sister what he had learned at Fukuda's dojo that day.

During the lessons, the eager and scientifically minded Kano pestered Fukuda for a detailed explanation of every technique—the exact placement of the hands and feet, the correct angle of entry, the proper distribution of weight, and so on—but Master Fukuda would usually lose patience quickly, saying, "Come here," and throw Kano repeatedly, until the inquisitive student gained practical knowledge through firsthand experience.

Another trainee at the dojo was a fellow named Aoki. Kano could soon hold his own against Aoki, and throw him regularly. However, Kano's main training partner and nemesis was a powerful heavyweight named Kanekichi Fukushima. Fukushima was not much of a technician—he didn't need to be because he was so big and strong. Since Fukushima stymied Kano in *randori* (freestyle competition), Kano asked a sumo wrestler friend for advice, hoping that sumo techniques would improve his performance. Sumo turned out to be of no help. Kano had a craftsman create a pair of dolls that Kano used to bend into different shapes and postures to see if he could solve the puzzle of how to throw Fukushima. Kano visited the National Library in Ueno to study anatomy manuals and to see what books on Western wrestling had to offer. There he formulated a technique he called the shoulder-wheel throw (*kata-guruma*). Since there was already a shoulder-throw technique in sumo known as *kinukazuki* as well as shoulder throws in several schools of jujutsu that Kano presumably knew about from his research into the traditional martial arts of Japan, Kano must have gotten a final hint for application of the throw from a European wrestling manual, perhaps the one published in Holland in the seventeenth century. Kano first tried out kata-guruma on Aoki. Since the technique worked well on Aoki, Kano employed it on Fukushima with the desired result—he finally threw the behemoth.

(Kano had a soft spot in his heart for Kanekichi Fukushima because he had learned so much with him as a partner. Sadly, Fukushima himself had an unhappy, tragic career. He was a fish wholesaler in the huge Tsukiji market, a rough and boisterous area. Fukushima had a number of memorable rows in his life— once trashing a district in the Yoshiwara pleasure quarter, and another time causing a riot during a festival at a Shinto shrine. He had been arrested several times. Evidently depressed at his bad behavior, Fukushima drowned himself in the Tamagawa River.)

In May 1879, Fukuda and Kano were among a select group of martial artists chosen to stage a demonstration for former United States president U. S. Grant when he visited Japan. The demonstrations, which included *kenjutsu* (swordsmanship) as well as jujutsu, were given in the garden of the home of businessman Eiichi Shibusawa, likely the richest private citizen in Japan at the time. The jujutsu demonstration consisted of *kata* forms (techniques practiced in arranged patterns) and randori. The demonstration was favorably received by General Grant and his party, and widely reported in the American press. Unfortunately, Kano's teacher Fukuda died four days after the demonstration at the age of fifty-one. Mrs. Fukuda gave Kano the transmission scrolls (texts containing the secrets of the ryu) left by her husband, and asked him to keep the dojo in operation. Kano attempted to do so but soon realized that he needed more training before assuming any kind of teaching duties.

Kano and Fukushima continued their study of jujutsu at the Tenjin Shin'yo ryu dojo of Masamoto Iso (1818–81), son of the school's founder. Since Masamoto was in his sixties at the time, he no longer engaged in randori, but he was still considered a master of kata. (Kano later told his own students that Masamoto's kata were "the most beautiful I ever saw executed.") Masamoto was highly skilled at atemi, and he also still possessed a cast-iron frame, able to withstand a direct blow to his body with a wooden sword. Kano gained proficiency in various kata under Masamoto's tutelage, and acquired extensive experience in randori as well; there were thirty students in Masamoto's dojo, and Kano, who was acting as assistant instructor of the dojo due to his previous experience in jujutsu, would have matches with all of them before the end of the day. Iso gave no instruction in randori, so Kano gained experience by actual participation rather than formal directions. Often he would not finish training until 11:00 P.M., and not infrequently he was overcome by fatigue on the way home. When he did manage to make it home, Kano refought the matches in his sleep, punching holes with his hands and feet in the paper doors in his room. He walked barefoot as much as possible, sometimes across gravel, to toughen his feet. To increase his strength and endurance on the way back from school, Kano carried huge kegs of pickled salmon from his father's house to share with his dormitory mates. To keep his training outfit from being torn to shreds, Kano patched it with strong kite string. The outfit, which still exists, is deeply stained from sweat and blood.

Just when Kano believed he was making good progress, he discovered that overconfidence is as dangerous as an opponent's techniques. One day near the end of the training session, a young stranger who had been observing practice for a few days asked Master Masamoto if he could join the training. When Masamoto gave him permission, the stranger borrowed a practice uniform, and then politely requested Kano to train with him. Even though tired out after the long training session, Kano agreed. Although the stranger was of ordinary build, seemingly a rank beginner, he countered Kano's throw and pinned him. While Kano was struggling to escape, the stranger suddenly let go. He bowed to Kano with a "Thank-you," and left the dojo, never to be seen again. Perhaps the stranger was a martial arts bodhisattva sent to teach Kano a lesson: "Never be overconfident or take anyone for granted."

Iso's dojo was not far from the famous Genbukan Hokushin Itto ryu dojo founded by Shusaku Chiba (1794–1856), a top kenjutsu master of the Bakumatsu period. It is believed that many students cross-trained in both jujutsu and kenjutsu at the two dojos. In those days, there could be throws and grappling in kenjutsu matches, and on occasion, the two kenjutsu fighters ended up on the ground wrestling in their full gear. Thus, kenjutsu students could use some knowledge of jujutsu.

In 1881, when Masamoto died, Kano was once more left without a teacher. This time he went to train with Tsunetoshi Iikubo (1835–89) of the Kito ryu. The pedigree of the Kito ryu dates back to the mid-seventeenth century. While the identity of the school's founder is in dispute, the Kito tradition was influenced by the teachings of the Yagyu school and those of Zen Master Takuan (1573–1645), lending it a more philosophical cast than that of the pragmatic Tenjin Shin'yo ryu. Originally the Kito ryu specialized in throws used when the combatants were in full armor, but in Kano's time the Kito ryu focused on throws based on the utilization of *ki* (cosmic energy) and timing. Unlike the two systems that Kano trained in previously, the Kito had far fewer kata, and twenty-one simple forms; the Kito ryu centered on perfectly timed throws rather than pure martial art techniques.

Regarding ki, here is an excerpt from the Kito ryu text *Densho Chusaku*:

Ki fulfills the body. When ki arises, it is called yang; when it is suppressed, it is called yin. In our system, we employ ki in the instruction of all the techniques, but ki is not a manifest object. If the body is not set aright, ki cannot be brought forth. Within everyday life, when one is in a sitting position, vigorous ki flourishes, and one becomes stable and secure. However, when techniques are executed with movements to the right or left, it adversely affects ki equilibrium. Ki pervades the body. Therefore, to set aright the body and correctly perceive ki everywhere is the tradition of our system. "Correctly" means through proper physical forms. The secret teaching of our system is this: continually polish your ki, do not be captivated by worldly objects, and keep firmly to the fundamentals. Do that, and when you execute the techniques, following the dictates of original ki, you can utilize ki and conduct yourself freely, right and left, back and forth. This is true for all aspects of life: stand, sit, move, or remain still in a state of natural ki. Heaven calls this Unshakable Wisdom.

Timing is described in this manner:

> In the Kito ryu, *ki* [a different ki than energy ki] means "rise,"
> and *to* means "fall." *Ki* is yang, *to* is yin. According to the cir-
> cumstance, utilize yang to attain victory; utilize yin to at-
> tain victory. When the opponent attacks with yin, use yang
> to win. When the opponent attacks with yang, use yin to
> emerge victorious. In our system, techniques are defined in
> terms of yin and yang. There are countless possible attacks
> and responses, but in actual combat situations, contrived
> strategy is mere distraction. Rely on the interplay of yin
> and yang to attain certain victory. A strong will with weak
> technique will not do; do not rely on your own strength but
> use your opponent's strength to achieve victory—this is the
> manner in which we employ ki [energy ki] in our system.
> Everything reverts back to this principle—abandon reliance
> on physical strength and obtain victory. If you abandon force
> and utilize ki, the opponent will defeat himself—this is the
> key to total victory. Transcend fixed patterns and learn the
> meaning of the saying "Mind over matter." If your heart is
> correct, your technique will be correct.

As can be seen from these two excerpts, in both style and content, the philosophical Kito ryu curriculum differed considerably
from that of the eminently practical Tenjin Shin'yo ryu. Kano
was pleased to be exposed to another perspective on jujutsu. Although in his fifties, Iikubo was big and strong, trained full-time,
and he could still best his young students in randori. He was
likely the most skilled martial artist under whom Kano trained.
(In his memoirs, Kano stated, "From Master Fukuda, I learned
what my life's work would be; from Master Masamoto, I learned
the subtle nature of *kata*; and from Master Iikubo, I learned varied techniques and the importance of timing.")

In regard to Kano's martial arts training, mention must be
made of the remarkable German physician Erwin Baelz (1849–
1913). In 1876, Baelz accepted a position with the Medical College

of Tokyo. He remained in Japan for twenty-seven years. In 1902, Baelz was appointed personal physician to the Emperor Meiji and the imperial household. Baelz also treated the prime ministers Hirobumi Ito and Yamagata Arimoto. Baelz trained hundreds of medical students during his tenure at the University of Tokyo, and was active on many other fronts.

Like Fenollosa, Dr. Baelz fell in love with Japanese culture. He collected art but, most important, promoted the continued practice of the traditional martial arts. In his book *Awakening Japan: The Diary of a German Doctor*, Baelz describes his infatuation with kenjutsu, *kyudo* (Japanese archery), and jujutsu. Baelz trained in kenjutsu with the master Kenkichi Sakakibara (1830–94) of the Jikishin-kage ryu, and in jujutsu with master Hikosuke Totsuka (1813–86), head of the Totsuka Ha Yoshin ryu based in Chiba Prefecture.

Like Kano, Baelz was appalled by the poor physical condition of the students attending higher schools in Japan. He thought that kendo and jujutsu training would be good additions to the regular curriculum as physical education. In 1880, Baelz persuaded the officials at the Tokyo University to hold a demonstration of jujutsu by the Totsuka Ha Yoshin ryu. According to Kano's own account, as a third-year student of Tokyo University, he was in attendance and impulsively ran down from the spectator seats to join in the freestyle matches. Kano wrote that he acquitted himself well with his impromptu performance. However, Baelz wrote that the Totsuka team routed Kano and the Kodokan members, but that is impossible since there was no Kodokan at the time. Kano was still a university student in the middle of his jujutsu training.

It is unclear exactly what relationship Baelz had with Kano and the Kodokan. At least in regard to Kano and the Kodokan, Baelz's memoirs are unreliable. In 1928, Kano visited Berlin. There he was shown a book entitled *Kano Jujutsu*, with a photo of Kano himself on the cover. Dr. Baelz had written the foreword. Kano had never seen the book before, or even heard of it. It was a German translation of *The Complete Kano Jiu-Jitsu* by H. Irving Hancock and Katsumi Higashi, published in 1904. Although Kano had

The Complete Kano Jiu-Jitsu by H. Irving Hancock and Katsumi Higashi

nothing to do with the book—see the inscription with Kano's disclaimer penned on the overleaf of the English edition (p. 16)—it was considered to be the authoritative judo textbook for the German police. Dr. Baelz's involvement with the book is unknown.

The Start of the Kodokan—and a Teaching Career

While he primarily trained in the three jujutsu schools mentioned above, Kano briefly studied *bojutsu* (stick fighting) at the Yagyu Shingen ryu dojo of Masateru Oshima. Oshima was a highly regarded martial arts master who taught jujutsu, bojutsu,

The inscription on the overleaf on the inside cover of *The Complete Kano Jiu-Jitsu* reads as follows: "This book says *The Complete Kano Jujitsu* but I should say this book teaches nothing of my Judo—This book explains in a way the teaching of one of the schools of jujitsu taught in Feudal Times in Japan which is now obliterated in Japan. Jigoro Kano."

and kenjutsu at his dojo. Kano also visited as many other martial arts masters as he could find. Fearful that their knowledge would be lost forever, some masters actually sought out Kano, who had gained a reputation for his serious research into the traditional martial arts. Sadly, nearly all were old, without disciples. Kano always asked, "Did the past masters of your ryu leave detailed instructions on the ideal way to win?" and "What type of advice did they give on the proper way to train?" They talked freely with

Kano about the techniques and philosophy of their respective ryu in the hope that he would preserve at least some of their teachings. A few gave him the transmission scrolls of their ryu, and Kano gathered other transmission scrolls from used-book stores and antiques shops. Kano had nearly one hundred transmission scrolls, not only from jujutsu ryu but from different schools of swordsmanship, archery, horsemanship, sumo, and many other martial arts traditions.

While training intently in jujutsu during the evenings, Kano pored over his books just as hard during the day. Kano graduated from Tokyo University in 1881, and then entered graduate school. While still in graduate school, Kano got a part-time teaching position at Gakushuin, the Peers School, in January 1882. In February of the same year, he established a private educational institution, the "Kano Academy."

At the end of February 1882, Kano decided he needed more space for himself and his students. He rented rooms at Eisho-ji, a small Jodo sect Buddhist temple in the Shimotani section of Tokyo. (With the Westernization of Japan, many temples in those days rented out rooms for extra income.)

On June 5, 1882, the twenty-two-year-old Kano formally established Kodokan judo. Kano had fallen in love with jujutsu and believed it must be preserved as a Japanese cultural treasure; however, he also believed it had to be adapted to modern times. He felt that no one ryu taught a complete system; each ryu had its own particularities and biases. Kano felt that the underlying principles of jujutsu should be systematized as Kodokan judo, a discipline of the mind and body that fostered wisdom and virtuous living. The official name of his institution was Nihon Den Kodokan Judo, "Institute for the Transmission of Japanese Judo." Comparing jujutsu to Hinayana Buddhism, a small vehicle with a limited vision, he equated Kodokan judo to Mahayana Buddhism, a big vehicle that embraced both individuals and society as a whole. "If the work of a human being does not benefit society," he declared, "that person's existence is in vain." As for the term *judo*, the "way of softness," it had been in use for several hundred

Kano at age twenty-two, the year he founded the Kodokan. Hereafter, there are few photographs of Kano dressed casually. He is seen dressed either like this, in a Western suit, or in formal Japanese attire—kimono or judo outfit.

years. Several old texts, for instance, defined *judo* "as the path that follows the flow of things," which in Kodokan judo Kano interpreted as the "most efficient use of energy."

(Even though Kodokan judo was established in 1882, for many years afterward his system was called "Kano ryu jujutsu" or simply "jujutsu" in many quarters. Actually, in the first year of the Kodokan's existence, Iikubo was still giving lessons to Kano and his students, so the emphasis was on Kito ryu jujutsu, not Kodokan judo, because there was no such thing yet. Kano wrote that it was not until 1877 that the technical base for Kodokan judo was formulated. In Europe and America in the early years, *jiujitsu* (jujutsu) and *jiudo* (judo) were used interchangeably. On the other hand, there were non-Kodokan jujutsu schools that appropriated the word *judo*. For example, *The Study of Judo*, published in 1925, lacks any mention of Kano or the Kodokan.)

Kano had two rooms for himself, one serving as a study. The other rooms were for his live-in students—and the largest room, twelve mats in size, doubled as the dojo. There were no set practice times. If someone showed up to train—in the morning, during the day, at night—the furniture was moved aside and the student trained with whomever was there.

The severity of the training began to take a toll on the building—floorboards were shattered, memorial tablets on the altar tumbled to the floor, and roof tiles were dislodged—so the head priest, Shunpo Asahi, demanded that Kano stop using rooms in the temple for a dojo. Thus, a small, makeshift twelve-mat dojo was built by one of the temple gates. Kano hung a sign on the small building: Kodokan, "Institute for Study of the Way."

Tsunejiro Tomita, Kano's first student, wrote in his journal of those early days:

Kano Sensei was only a few years older than we were, so he trained just as hard if not harder than we did. He was driven, training whenever he had a spare moment from his teaching duties. He was constantly experimenting and refining the techniques using us as punching bags. From morning to night, it was judo, judo, judo. We drank mugi tea with a bit of sugar in it, and ate rice seasoned only with lotus roots from the temple pond. Mostly I remember being sleepy and hungry, but I never thought of running away.

As for his own studies, Kano undertook a simultaneous investigation of Western sports such as wrestling and boxing while continuing his research into the classical martial art systems of Japan based on both practical experience and theory. As noted above, being only slightly older than the trainees, Kano practiced just as intently as they did. He had to. As will be discussed later, Kano had his hands full trying to handle his students, especially Shiro Shida (Saigo).

In July 1882, Kano completed his graduate studies at Tokyo University. Kano was hired as a full-time instructor at Gakushuin in August 1882 and launched his parallel career as a professional educator.

At Gakushuin he was appalled at the students' bad behavior. The student body at that time was made up of the spoiled children of aristocrats. (The future emperor Taisho studied there later.) The students rode to school in rickshaws and had the drivers carry their books into the school. They were lazy and rude, and treated the teachers like servants. Kano changed all that. "I don't care who your parents are. Shape up or ship out!" The students listened. Since teacher Kano had been training intensely in the martial arts for years, he looked as if he meant business.

During the first days of the Kodokan, Kano took in a fellow named Shirai to accommodate one of his father's friends. Shirai was a former military man who was nice enough when sober, but violent and difficult to handle when he had a few drinks (that is why he was sent to Kano). When Shirai became rough and abusive—he even tried to punch Kano on occasion—Kano would pin him, "gently and kindly," and wait patiently for Shirai to calm down. Gradually, Shirai learned to gain some control over his drinking, convincing Kano of the value of a gentle and kind judo.

An acquaintance of Kano, Genzo Murata, asked Kano to set up a Tokyo office for his new company, Nihon Kosasha. At first it was to be an office in name only, so Kano could use a building to house both the office and his Kobunkan English Academy. In February 1883, a house was found in Minami Jimbo-cho. Kano used the storehouse that was attached to the property as a dojo. The place was hardly ideal for a dojo—it was dank and cold, was obstructed by support pillars, and had a hard floor. Kano only had ten mats, which he brought from Eisho-ji. Since it was inconvenient for most students to attend training during the week, the dojo was kept open on weekdays from 3:00 P.M. to 7:00 P.M. and on Sundays from 7:00 A.M. to noon. As instructor, Kano had to be continually on hand, even if it was freezing cold (the storehouse was unheated) and no students showed up. If Kano

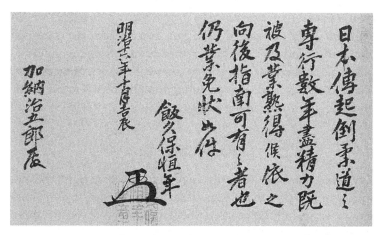

Kito ryu transmission license bestowed on Kano by Tsunetoshi Iikubo. "After years of diligent practice and understanding of the techniques of Dai Nihon Den Kito Judo, you are fully qualified to hereafter act as an instructor and I therefore present you with a Transmission License. [signed] Iikubo Tsunetoshi. Meiji 16 [1883], October, an auspicious day. [Presented to] Kano Jigoro." The significant point is that Iikubo called his school "Dai Nihon Den Kito Judo," not "Jujutsu."

could not make it, his top student, Saigo, was on duty. On many occasions, only the two of them were there. Even though they trained vigorously, they could not warm up, and their feet were always frozen. These were the darkest days of the Kodokan's existence.

Kano's teacher Iikubo continued to visit the dojo once or twice a week, as he did at Eisho-ji, to give instruction, stopping by on the way home from his job at the postal service. Iikubo sauntered to the dojo samurai style, neatly decked out, carrying a heavy iron fan in his sash in case ruffians attacked him. Iikubo dominated Kano as usual. Then, one day in 1883, Kano grasped the key to judo—"If my partner pulls, I push; if he pushes, I pull." Kano of course knew this as a theory, but now he had actually and truly experienced it in both body and mind. Kano threw Iikubo three times in succession. Kano ascribed this breakthrough not to any mystical experience—as was (and is) often the case with many martial artists—but rather to years of careful investigation, a rational approach to the art, and tireless experimentation with his own trainees. Iikubo bestowed a formal Kito ryu teaching license on Kano in the autumn of 1883, gave him the Kito ryu transmission scrolls, and presented him with a *keikogi* (training uniform), which Kano thereafter continued to wear for years. Nonetheless, Kano still had a hard time attracting students owing to his youth and lack of proper training facilities.

Life at the Kodokan

Only nine students formally registered in 1884, eight the following year, and ten the year after that, making a total of only twenty-seven fully committed Kodokan students in the first three years of its existence.

In September 1883, Kano moved to Kami-Nibancho in Kojimachi and built a small dojo of ten mats on the grounds of his rented residence. Fortunately, more students joined the Kodokan, so Kano turned another larger room into a twenty-mat dojo. The dojo was open every afternoon from 2:00 to 11:00 P.M. Kano would come out to teach whenever anyone came to train. In 1884, *kagami-biraki*, the opening ceremony of the New Year, was established. A ranking system came into being—at the incipient stage, there were three basic levels (*kyu*), and three advanced ranks (*dan*). Tomita and Saigo, the initial two full-time live-in trainees, were the first to be presented with the rank of first dan. A regular day of open competition was established once a month, and two *kohaku* (red versus white team competitions) were set up for spring and autumn. Kano instituted *kan-geiko*, "cold-weather training," thirty days of severe midwinter practice between four and seven in the morning. (In 1896, *shochu-geiko*, "midsummer training," the steamy counterpart to the frigid midwinter training, was introduced.)

Kano also established the Kodokan Oath, which he wanted each member of the dojo to sign with a seal of blood:

1. Hereafter, I promise to wholeheartedly persevere in Judo and shall not quit training for any unwarranted reason.

2. I promise not to bring dishonor on the dojo in any way.
3. I promise that I will not reveal the secret arts of Judo by either visual or verbal means to anyone without authorization.
4. I promise not to instruct others in the art of Judo without authorization.
5. As a student, and later if I obtain an instructor license, I promise to always follow Judo rules.

Nine students officially placed their names together with a seal of blood on the initial Kodokan register book in 1884: Tsunejiro Yamada (later adopted into the Tomita family) and Shiro Shida (Saigo), the first two live-in disciples; Seiko Higuchi, tenth-generation head of the Higuchi clan, later a viscount and member of the House of Peers; Sumiaki Arima, also from an aristocratic family, Kano's third live-in student, military officer, and finally an important official in the imperial household; Tamakichi Nakajima, later dean of the Kyoto University Law School; Toraomaro Matsuoka, later professor of physical education at the Peers School; Sumitomo Arima, later educator and judo instructor, author of *Japanese Physical Culture, Being a Further Exposition of Jiujutsu and Similar Arts*, published in English in 1908; Genjiro Amano, pioneer in the development of Hokkaido, and later founder of the Osaka Hotel (Kano described him as very keen, but sometimes a danger to himself and others, including Kano, by overdoing it); and Keijiro Kawai, who is described as "being tremendously strong."

Although not on the original register—it is thought that there were about twenty students studying at the Kodokan at that time but for various reasons only nine signed the register—Takejiro Yuasa was raised and educated by Kano. Yuasa and his widowed mother entered the Kano Academy at the same time. Mrs. Yuasa helped with the day-to-day chores of running the Kano Academy. Tiny Mrs. Yuasa was as strong as any of the young students—she could lift a one hundred–pound bag of rice with one hand while using a broom in the other. She was once featured in a newspaper article called "The Powerhouse Housekeeper." The students loved her for passing them treats, but she was known to turn them away on occasion with the words "Don't be greedy." Take-jiro Yuasa is listed on the second register.

During this period, the regimen of a live-in student at the Kano Academy—most of whom Kano supported entirely out of his own pocket—was as austere as that of any monk. (In fact, Kano based the schedule and training rules on those of a strictly run Buddhist temple that he had once visited.) A live-in student had to rise at 4:40 A.M. and immaculately clean his room, the buildings, and the grounds. The day was strictly divided into periods of book study (philosophy, political science, economics, and psychology), calligraphy and painting practice, and judo training in the evenings from 5:00 to 6:30 P.M. (Many of the students attended school elsewhere during the day.) While studying—or listening to Kano's formal lectures—the trainees had to wear a kimono with *hakama* (pleated pants) and sit in *seiza*. Kano tended to be long-winded, so sometimes the students had to sit for two hours on the hard floor. When not training or studying, the students were kept busy fetching water from the well, looking after guests, cleaning up after meals, and preparing the bath. The day ended at 9:30 P.M. Food was simple: soup, rice, pickles, vegetables, tofu, bamboo shoots, and salted fish. The rooms were unheated (because you were supposed to be cold in winter and heat was an unnecessary luxury). The students were allowed to visit home twice a month, on the second and fourth Sundays, and it was said that they'd race out the door on those Sunday mornings and return at the very last moment that night.

The students had to sign an oath to always show proper respect and consideration to the teacher, to one another, and to guests. And promise not to nap or daydream! Kano instituted this rule because teachers at the various schools that Kano's students were attending during the day complained that Kano's charges were so tired from getting up early that they were dozing off in class. One student later recollected that he even fell asleep while walking to school.

In addition, Kano tutored the academy students on handling money, dressing appropriately, and proper behavior in public. Kano instructed the students to go on foot wherever they were headed, moving at a fast clip, and not rely on public transportation. At first, all the money sent from their parents went directly to Kano. He made sure the money was used wisely, and not wasted. Later, he did start giving the students small allowances. He told them they must become international citizens by maintaining the best traditions and high culture of Japan. Kano and the students met for tea once a week; every Saturday night there was a book club; and there were long outdoor walks, usually an excursion to some historical site, scheduled on the first and third Sunday afternoons, and holidays. On those Sunday nights, there were group meetings for general discussion and research reports by individual students. During summer break, Kano and the students went to the seashore to swim and relax a bit. Also, there were baseball games once in a while, and field days with running and calisthenics. The motto of Kano's academy was "Do it yourself," and all students were responsible for washing and mending their uniforms. Kano's own schedule was the same, with the added burden of often sitting up all night to do translation work for the Ministry of Education in order to make ends meet.

There were regular small welcome, farewell, and celebration parties, so the students did have an occasional chance to eat cakes, fruits, and other snacks—in winter, baked sweet potatoes were a favorite. And boys will be boys. There were always a few who would sneak out at night and fool around if the chance presented itself. On the other hand, there was a group of students who secretly went to practice Zazen at a temple. They wanted more meditative fare than was being served at the staunchly Confucian Kano Academy.

(The Kano Academy closed in 1919. One reason was Kano's age, and the other was, "Times change. Students aren't as keen as they used to be." Over the years, more than three hundred pupils studied at the Kano Academy. Nearly all of them rose to the top of their profession, whether it be education, business, medicine, the military, or government service. Regarding his academy students, Kano remarked, "The students sent to me from rich families were usually spoiled, willful, and lazy. It was my job to

Kano, age twenty-five.

whip them into shape, and they didn't like it. I had to be tough on them. Other academy students came from extremely poor backgrounds. They were grateful to have a roof over their heads. Such students were the hardest working and never complained.")

During this period, Kano was also practicing judo a lot outside the dojo. He was obliged to use a horse often in those days to get around, but he never got the hang of horseback riding. Thanks to his judo breakfall training, however, he managed to land safely on his feet each time a horse threw him.

By 1885, the number of applicants had increased to fifty-four. Since none of the Kodokan judo men at the time could be described as hefty, Kano actually tried to recruit a few heavy-weights—without much success. Since men of large bulk had a difficult time moving quickly, and could easily be beaten by much smaller men in contests with rules, continuing such training held little appeal for them.

In the spring of 1886, Kano moved his residence again, this time to Fujimi-cho. Yajiro Shinagawa, the newly appointed ambassador to England, asked Kano to "house-sit." Kano built a nice forty-mat dojo on the property. Ninety-nine students registered that year. At the Fujimi-cho dojo, students with dan rankings first began wearing black belts as a sign of their status. It was during the three-year period at the Fujimi-cho dojo that Kano, working closely with his instructors, Tomita, Saigo, Yoshitsugu Yamashita, and Sakujiro Yokoyama, formulated the basic technical aspects of Kodokan judo.

Contest Judo

During this period, Kano divided Kodokan judo into three aspects: physical education judo; forging the spirit judo; and contest judo. Physical education judo was centered on the practice of fixed forms and other exercises to build a fit and healthy body. Forging the spirit judo was based on ethics: how to foster the development of respect, good manners, courtesy, attentiveness, and so forth. Contest judo was lab work, an activity in which practitioners could test their technical judo skills. The primary aim of Kodokan judo was to build character, not superior competition fighters.

Despite such noble aims, the two events that helped put Kodokan judo on the map were fiercely competitive: the open tournaments sponsored by the National Police Agency under the direction of Superintendent-General Michitsune Mishima (1835–88).

The rules of this tournament were more civilized than previous open contests, which were essentially free-for-alls. In fact, open contests were such deadly serious affairs that, as a precaution, competitors in such battles bade farewell to their parents and friends before setting out for combat. The rules generally favored the Kodokan competitors because the most effective jujutsu techniques—which were meant to be lethal—were prohibited due to the grave danger involved.

There are various accounts of the nature of the contests and when they were held. May 1885 or June 1886 are the two dates most often cited for the first tournament. Depending on the source, between five and ten matches were scheduled, with fighters of different schools facing off against each other. The main competition was between the Totsuka Ha Yoshin ryu and the Kodokan. The Kodokan team won or tied the matches between the two groups, but the crucial contests were the last two. Demon Yokoyama of the Kodokan was pitted against Demon-Slayer Nakamura of the Totsuka Ha Yoshin ryu. Nakamura was so shocked by an earlier defeat a few years previously at the hands of Tomita that he gave up drinking, and trained much more earnestly than before. Powerful Nakamura was in the best shape of his life. The first thirty minutes of the match was a standoff; the men barely moved from the center of the mat, and neither was able to throw the other. The match went to the ground for the next twenty-five minutes and was finally declared a draw. The men's hands had to be pried apart because they had been gripping each other so tightly. (Yokoyama later wrote that he thought that he was going to die during the match.)

Regarding the next match, here is the testimony of Tsunejiro Tomita in an article entitled "Yama-arashi and Saigo," which appears in the June 1931 edition of the journal *Judo*:

The last contest was between Saigo representing the Kodokan against Terushima Taro from the Totsuka Ha Yoshin ryu. Terushima had the best of it in the early going, tossing the much smaller Saigo—Terushima was nearly ten inches taller and fifty pounds heavier—in the air. However, the extremely agile Saigo always landed on his feet. (Two of Saigo's nicknames were "Cat" and "Octopus Toes." "Cat" because after carefully observing the motions a cat uses to land on its feet even when thrown high in the air, Saigo practiced such turning motions by jumping from the second floor of a building. "Octopus Feet," because his toes were unnaturally turned in so his feet stuck to any surface.) During the contest Saigo, suddenly applied a devastating technique immortalized as *yama-arashi* (mountain storm), flipping Terushima down for the victory. Saigo's victory carried the day, and both his reputation and that of the Kodokan was established.

The exact nature of Saigo's *yama-arashi* technique has always been debated. Tomita wrote that Saigo's yama-arashi was a unique, one-of-a-kind maneuver, not a particular technique. That singular yama-arashi was the result of optimal conditions (certain techniques are much easier when one's opponent is taller with longer arms), perfect timing, complete presence of body and mind (*kiai*), and precise movement. Thereafter, Saigo's application of yama-arashi was subtly different each time he executed it. As Tomita wrote, "Before Saigo, no *yama-arashi*; after Saigo, no *yama-arashi*."

Another National Police Agency tournament seems to have been held in 1888. In Yoshitsugu Yamashita's account, it was Saigo defeating Totsuka Ha Yoshin ryu fighter Entaro Kochi with yama-arashi ("Account of the First Generation of Kodokan Judo versus Jujutsu Matches," *King Magazine*, October 1929). In this tournament, it was Yamashita who was victorious over Terushima Taro. The eyewitness account left by Itsuro Munakata also describes the contest as between Saigo and Kochi, with Saigo winning by his devastating yama-arashi technique (*Sekai Judo Shi*, 1974).

In any event, Saigo certainly defeated one or the other (or both) Totsuka Ha Yoshin ryu fighters with his yama-arashi technique. After Saigo had used his famed yama-arashi throw in public a few times, competitors naturally set to work developing countertechniques. Saigo once had a match with Shusaburo Sano, a large powerhouse also from the Totsuka Ha Yoshin ryu. Sano was said to be able to bend iron rods with his arms and shatter thick boards with his fists. Sano outweighed Saigo by sixty pounds. During the match, Sano was able to counter Saigo's expected yama-arashi throw and come down on Saigo with his full weight, immediately applying a pin. However, Saigo slipped out of the pin in a flash (like a cat) and applied a counterlock on Sano's arm, forcing him to tap out. Perhaps the whole thing was a ploy by Saigo to let Sano think he was actually countering yama-arashi.

While the Kodokan team won most of the matches against the Totsuka Ha Yoshin ryu team, there was one group of jujutsu men, from the Fusen ryu, led by head master Mataemon Tanabe (1869–1942), that handily defeated Kodokan men in contests. The Fusen ryu founder, Soto Zen monk Motsugai Takeda (1795–1867), was one of the most physically powerful martial artists in Japanese history, said to have possessed near superhuman strength, able to lift heavy temple bells; uproot trees; win at tugs-of-war, with only Motsugai himself against dozens of opponents; move huge boulders blocking a road; and so on. His nickname was "Monk Fist." Once Motsugai found a nice Go board that he wanted to purchase from an antiques shop. Motsugai had no money with him at the time, so the shopkeeper asked for some kind of deposit. Motsugai struck the hard surface of the board with his fist, leaving indentations of knuckles. "Will that do?" Motsugai asked. Thereafter, instead of getting a sample of calligraphy from Motsugai—he was a well-known Zen artist—people would ask him to "sign" their thick Go boards with his trademark knuckle marks.

Ironically, the fourth-generation head master of the Fusen ryu, Tanabe, was a small, thin man, with little raw physical strength. Nevertheless, Tanabe had engaged in thousands of matches in his career against all kinds of jujutsu men, sumo wrestlers, and street brawlers. Because he was so small and no match for his opponents' physical strength, he could not hope to throw them. Instead, by "practicing catching eels in my bare hands and watching snakes swallow frogs," he developed into an incomparable grappler on the ground. Keeping low, he worked to trip up his opponent; as soon as the match was on the ground, it was all over for Tanabe's opponent, by either a joint lock or a choke.

As usual, accounts of matches between the Kodokan and the

Fusen ryu differ. One has Tanabe challenging the Kodokan men at the kagami-biraki of the Osaka Branch. He roundly defeated them all, and Kano himself supposedly refused to accept the challenge. In 1900, at an exhibition match before the crown prince, Tanabe defeated a Kodokan man with a leg lock. At any rate, all agree that the even the highest-ranking Kodokan competitors could not handle the Fusen ryu fighters on the ground. Typically, Kano realized from the defeat of his Kodokan men how weak they were on the ground, and thus employed Tanabe to work with students in order to improve their grappling techniques. Kano reluctantly adopted much of Tanabe's Fusen ryu groundwork into Kodokan judo, eliminating Tanabe's alarming training principle: "Never submit, never surrender."

Kano also incorporated groundwork from other jujutsu schools into Kodokan judo, mostly because he did not want his men to look bad in open competitions. Kano never liked groundwork. He said, "Human beings were made to walk, not crawl." He thought groundwork largely detrimental to Kodokan judo— grappling on the ground quickly degenerated into unseemly schoolyard wrestling. It was undignified. Furthermore, there was a much greater possibility of getting injured in groundwork because of the severity of application, and subsequent resistance to, chokes and pins. In addition, groundwork is only good against one opponent. If there is more than one opponent, there is no possibility of grappling one-to-one on the ground. Fighters have to stay on their feet to deal with multiple attackers. There is a saying, "To learn throwing techniques well, it takes three years; to learn effective groundwork, it takes three months." To Kano, groundwork was the easy way out. For Kano, ideal judo was comprised of at least 70 percent standing techniques and no more than 30 percent groundwork.

Kano Refines Judo and Travels Abroad

All these matches with other ryu, win or lose, taught both Kano and his students important lessons for the further refinement of their techniques. Kano believed that each victory reaffirmed that their approach was in the right direction; each defeat was a wake-up call. Looking back on the early days of the Kodokan, one sees that the primary emphasis was on throws, but gradually, as a result of cross-training with other schools, more groundwork, joint locks, and pinning and choking techniques were added. Old-style jujutsu schools—full of die-hard, fight-to-the-finish, no-holds-barred martial artists—were no match for Kano's carefully thought out, well-planned, and more humane Kodokan system. That is the reason Kodokan judo became preeminent over jujutsu styles, not because of the number of victories in open contests.

The Kodokan began to attract larger numbers of trainees. In 1886, 98 people enrolled; in 1887, 292; in 1888, 378; and in 1889, 605 new students registered.

In April 1888, Kano, together with the Reverend T. Lindsay, delivered a paper—and presumably a demonstration—on "Jujutsu" to the members of the Asiatic Society of Japan, a study group consisting of English-speaking foreign diplomats, professors, and businessmen. In the paper, the authors contended that while there is evidence of certain Japanese martial arts being influenced by Chinese boxing, jujutsu is of purely native origin. The paper illustrated the principle of *ju* (flexibility in body and mind) by relating the tale of an old-time teacher observing willow branches yielding, but not breaking, under the weight of heavy snow. It also contained stories of famous masters of jujutsu, including that of Jushin Sekiguchi (1597–1676). One day while Sekiguchi was accompanying his lord across a narrow bridge, the lord decided to test the jujutsu master by suddenly shoving him to the edge. Sekiguchi seemed to yield, putting up no resistance, but at the last second he slipped around and had to save the lord from being catapulted headfirst into the water.

In April 1889, the Kodokan moved into an unused military barracks in Hongo Masago-cho, and the Kano Academy was moved to Kojimachi in in Kami-Nibancho. The Kodokan had a seventy-mat dojo, and the Kojimachi branch dojo had forty mats.

There were more than fifteen hundred full-time students, and several branches of the Kodokan at different police and military academies and universities. Kano's Kodokan judo was on its way to assuming a preeminent position in the martial arts world of modern Japan.

In August of the same year, Kano resigned his position at Gakushuin—he didn't get along with the new principal, Goro Miura, a former general who wanted Gakushuin to be a military academy—and at the request of the Imperial Household Agency, he prepared to embark on a long inspection tour of the educational institutions in Europe. Kano left his senior disciples Tomita and Saigo in charge of the Kodokan. Accompanied by a member of the Imperial Household Agency, Kano set sail from Yokohama on September 15, 1889. With few people from Japan traveling overseas at that time, Kano and his companion were the only two Japanese passengers on board.

After stopping in Shanghai, they arrived in Marseilles in October. Over the next year, Kano visited Lyons, Paris, Brussels, Berlin, Vienna, Copenhagen, Stockholm, Amsterdam, The Hague, Rotterdam, and London; on the return trip, he stopped off at Cairo to view the pyramids. In Europe, Kano was most impressed by the cleanliness and order of the villages, and the beauty and individual character of each house. In the cities, it was the large number of huge buildings and cathedrals, and their gargantuan scale. At first, Kano believed religion to be the pervasive force in European society. After talking with the Europeans themselves and observing their behavior, however, he concluded that while religion had once held sway, European society was—like Japan— becoming more and more secular.

Kano was further impressed with the frugality of many Europeans, who, like the Japanese, were careful not to waste anything. The virtue of frugality was one of Kano's principal beliefs: in judo as well as daily life, one should always strive for the most efficient use of objects and energy. He also noted that while the Japanese students who studied foreign languages were hesitant to speak or write for fear of committing a blunder, native speakers often garbled the syntax of their own language and sent him letters full of spelling mistakes. That was not the ideal, of course, but it did prove to Kano that Japanese students should not be overly concerned about making errors when learning to speak or write a foreign language. All in all, Kano enjoyed his first visit to Europe very much, and he felt that there would be no problem with Japanese and Europeans associating on friendly terms.

Having visited Egypt in the company of an Englishman, a Frenchman, a Dutchman, a Swiss, and an Austrian, Kano proudly reported to his friends back in Japan that he alone was able to race to the top of a pyramid and back down without requiring any assistance, water, or even a break to rest. During the long return voyage, Kano discussed judo with his follow passengers, and demonstrated its efficacy. Since there was a boastful strongman Russian sailor reputed to be a champion wrestler on board, a challenge match was arranged, for want of better entertainment. Even though the sailor got a good grip on Kano, the judo master was able to improvise a technique—half *koshi-nage*, half *seio-nage*—and throw his opponent. What impressed the crowd of passengers the most was not the ability of the smaller man to throw the larger, but the fact that Kano held the big sailor in a manner that kept him from being injured when he hit the deck. As can be imagined, the incident was reported favorably in the Japanese press.

In addition to this throwing match, Kano and the sailor reportedly engaged in an "I-can-pin-you, you-can't-pin-me" contest. Again, Kano prevailed.

While the ship was docked in Saigon, Kano took a stroll through the city. On the outskirts of town, he was suddenly surrounded by a pack of wild dogs. If it had been a group of thugs, Kano would not have been worried, but the barking dogs threw him. He realized that if he tried to fight them off, the dogs would become more frantic and aggressive, so he used judo. That is, when he kept his composure and remained calm, the dogs quieted down.

Kano returned to Japan in mid-January 1891. He had been abroad for sixteen months. There was no place for him to live, so he stayed with his sister Katsuko Yanagi for a time. The Kodokan was suddenly required to vacate the army barracks in Masago-cho, so everything was moved to the Kojimachi branch dojo in Kami-Nibancho.

Unfortunately, rambunctious Saigo had gotten into serious trouble while Kano was in Europe. As mentioned above, during the early days of the Kodokan, some members continued to visit rival schools in order to test their skills. Chief among them was Saigo, who, along with some of his Kodokan pals, had taken to loitering around busy street corners in bad neighborhoods ready to challenge all comers. One day, Saigo and his gang were confronted by a group of sumo wrestlers, headed by the behemoth Araumi, "Stormy Sea." Araumi made short work of the other Kodokan fighters, leaving diminutive Saigo to meet the challenge. Though tipsy with sake, Saigo managed to down his man. However, when the giant wrestler sank his teeth deep into Saigo's shin, Saigo knocked Araumi unconscious. A bloody free-for-all among the sumo wrestlers and judo men quickly ensued, the police were summoned, and the entire party was hauled off to jail. To complicate matters, Saigo had injured several police officers during the melee. The other members of the Kodokan were able to get Saigo released from detention, but when Kano was informed of the incident, he had no choice but to banish his most talented student for "Infractions against the Rules of the Kodokan."

Kano Marries and the Kodokan Grows

In 1891, the thirty-one-year-old Kano decided it was time to marry, and after seeking an appropriate match with the help of acquaintances, he wed Sumako Takezoe, daughter of the poet and diplomat Shinichiro Takezoe, on August 7. Alas, Kano was obliged to leave his new bride behind the following month when he assumed the position of principal at the Fifth Higher School in remote Kumamoto.

Kano and Sumako on their wedding day, 1891. Notice Kano's coat, hat, and sword, the outfit of a European aristocrat. Kano was thirty-one at the time.

As is always the case, educational innovation lags behind in the provinces, and Kano viewed his new job at the Fifth Higher School as a special challenge. The budget was meager, the facilities poor, and the teachers insufficiently trained. And neither was there a dojo. Without sufficient funds to build one, Kano and his judo students were forced to practice outdoors but later got the use of a hall for a dojo called Zuihokan. Kano had brought a Kodokan judo disciple named Soji Kimotsuki with him to help teach, and Junshin Arima arrived later as a formal instructor at the school.

The political situation in Kumamoto was unstable. At a Kokumin Kyokai Party convention that Kano was attending, a riot broke out, with Kano stuck in the middle. Unbeknownst to Kano, one of his judo trainees named Shirakawa, disguised as a student, had followed his teacher into the hall to protect him (as if Kano needed protecting) in case of trouble. Both got out safely.

One of the new teachers hired at the school at Kano's personal request was Lafcadio Hearn (1850–1904). Later to achieve worldwide renown as a writer, Hearn wrote an essay on "Jujutsu" that appeared in his book *Out of the East*, first published in 1892. The rambling essay says very little about Kano or judo, but it does make the point that Japan should rely on the spirit of judo—flexible yet firm—when dealing with Western powers. In his memoirs, Kano mentions a rather elaborate ceremony in town. All of the other participants were decked out in Western-style frock coats, dresses, or military uniforms save one—Lafcadio Hearn in a formal Japanese kimono. And while everyone else was staring directly toward the camera, Hearn was facing completely to one side, so as to show his best profile.

In 1893, the Ministry of Education called Kano to back to Tokyo. Kano resumed living with his wife, Sumako, and at the end of the year their first child, Noriko, a daughter, was born. (The couple went on to have eight children in all, five girls and three boys.)

From 1889 to 1893, Kano was absent from the Kodokan, first overseas and then in Kumamoto. While Kano was away, the Kodokan membership grew substantially, but with the consequence that Kano had less and less contact with more and more students. Further, the teaching load was distributed among his instructors, some of whom were not Kano's direct students and thus not well versed in Kano's Kodokan philosophy.

In December 1893, a fine 107-mat dojo was opened in Koishikawa Shimotomizaka-cho. The Kano Academy also relocated there. The official grand opening, on May 20, 1894, was not at all an exclusive Kodokan judo show. Included were demonstrations of kata by representatives of many other styles. Here is the lineup:

Kata Demonstrations

Kodokan Judo Nage-Kata: Yoshitsugu Yamashita and Norimasu Iwasaki

Kodokan Judo Itsutsu-no-Kata: Tsunejiro Tomita and Katsutaro Oda

Kito Ryu: Jigoro Kano and Yoshitsugu Yamashita

Takenouchi Santo Ryu: Masaaki Samura, partner unknown

Ryoi Shinto Ryu: Hansuke Nakamura and Shogo Uehara

Shibukawa Ryu: Tetsutaro Hisatomi, partner unknown

Tenjin Shin'yo Ryu: Keitaro Inoue and Takisaburo Tobari

Jikishin Ryu: Tamihei Iwasaki, partner unknown

Randori Demonstrations

Yoshin Ryu Shintaro Katayama versus Keishi Ryu Kinosuke Nomura

Yoshin Ryu Kinsaku Yamamoto versus Kodokan Judo Takeo Hirose

Tobari Ryu Eizo Yamaguchi versus Kodokan Judo Yuji Hirooka

Takenouchi Ryu Kotaro Imai versus Kodokan Judo Soji Kimotsuki

Hokuso Ryu Shizo Inamura versus Takenouchi Ryu Senjuro Kataoka

Hokuso Ryu Ichiji Kono versus Kodokan Judo Takisaburo Tobari

All had a splendid time.

For the first time, Kano reluctantly instituted a nominal monthly dojo fee for members of the Kodokan. Heretofore, Kano had assumed almost the entire financial burden of the Kodokan operating expenses, support of his live-in disciples, traveling expenses for himself and his instructors, and other costs. He was not "teaching Kodokan judo for money. I teach Kodokan judo as a Way of Life." However, such a noble attitude, in which he never faltered, kept Kano broke all his life.

In 1894, the Sino-Japanese War erupted. The subsequent war fever—which Kano did nothing to encourage—made the practice of judo more popular. Japan was involved in another war in 1904–5, this time with Russia. In this Russo-Japanese War, Kano lamented the loss of a number of senior Kodokan members in battle, including his close students, commanders Yuasa and Hirose. Kano warned his countrymen against developing false confidence because of Japan's heady victories over China in 1898 and Russia in 1905. China, burdened with a hopelessly corrupt imperial court and ineffectual army, more or less defeated itself; Russia was unable to supply the distant Far Eastern front with sufficient men or materiel, and if the war had been waged closer to Moscow, the outcome could have been much different. "War is never a good thing," Kano wrote, "and continual warmongering will eventually lead to defeat for any country."

In 1906, the Kodokan expanded again, this time to a specially built 207-mat dojo. The opening ceremony for the new building was held on March 23 and 24, 1907, again with demonstrations by many various ryu.

The card this time:

Kata Demonstrations

Toda Ryu: Mamoru Yatani and Yasaburo Itozakura

Jikishin Ryu: Iaido demonstration by Empei Itozaki

Iga Ryu: Hikozo Akaishi and Tetsunosuke Onizawa

Yoshin Ryu: Hidemi Tozuka and Kinsaku Yamamoto

Takenouchi Ryu: Kunio Murakami and Shin Nishimura

Sekiguchi Ryu: Tadaaki Nisshi and Bo Uchiyama

Kiraku Ryu: Mamoru Yatani and Yasaburo Itozakura

Kito Ryu: Jigoro Kano and Yoshitsugu Yamashita

Randori Demonstrations (All Kodokan Judo Men)

Gensui Arai (third dan) versus Itsuyo Sawa (third dan)

Keigen Otsuno (third dan) versus Tokisaburo Karino (third dan)

Yoshio Fukunaga (third dan) versus Jun Deguchi (third dan)

Tetsu Suzuki (fourth dan) versus Nobushiro Satake (fourth dan)

Shuichi Nagaoka (sixth dan) versus Kunisaburo Iizuka (fifth dan)

Yoshitsugu Yamashita (seventh dan) versus Hajime Isogai (sixth dan)

Since it is evident from the number of demonstrations by different ryu in both opening ceremonies and by the many prefaces Kano wrote for various jujutsu training manuals that Kano continued to support the old-style jujutsu schools throughout his career, the rivalry between Kodokan judo and the traditional jujutsu ryu has perhaps been overstated. In 1911, Kano wrote the preface for the training manual of the Shinshin Takuma ryu. (The name means "With a mind free of the four concerns—about one's body, one's life, one's death, and one's foes—train long and hard.") In the preface, Kano states his view of the role of the traditional jujutsu schools:

> Although the approach and techniques of this jujutsu system differ from that of the Kodokan, it is important to preserve such traditional ryu from a research perspective. We can compare which points are the same and which points are different. The study and preservation of the traditional jujutsu systems of Japan is a worthwhile and necessary pursuit.

Around the time of the opening of the new dojo, the *judogi* (practice uniform) was standardized in the form we see today. (In the old days, the pants were often quite short, and the jackets quilted in different patterns.)

Kano's Career as an Educator

It is remarkable that Kano was able to accomplish so much—develop Kodokan judo into an international organization and establish universal physical education in Japan all the while being employed as a full-time educator. Actually, it was double- or triple-time, since he concurrently held at least one other official appointment and, from 1922, served as a member of the House of Peers.

Kano's first job upon graduation in 1882 was as an instructor at the Peers School. Thereafter, in addition to operating his own private academies, Kano held a bewildering series of joint appointments as professor, visiting professor, or principal at the Peers School, Komaba College, Jinjo College, Tokyo Women's Higher School, the Fifth Higher School in Kumamoto, the Nada Middle School in Kobe, and all kinds of positions at the Ministry of Education.

On top of all this, Kano was the director of an academy for Chinese exchange students. The Ch'ing dynasty was crumbling, and conditions in China were hardly ideal. Kano, who had opened a private academy for Chinese exchange students in 1896, was asked by the Japanese minister of education Saionji to establish a larger academy in the hope that the students could get a "breath of fresh air" and return to assist in the modernization of their homeland. Thus, the Kobun Gakuen came into being. Kano was appointed director, and moved into a house located next to the academy. In 1902, Kano embarked for China on an official inspection tour of that nation's educational institutions. He met with government officials to discuss the modernization of education in China. Kano communicated with his Chinese counterparts through the written language that was the same for both countries even though the spoken languages were completely different. When he wasn't in meetings with officials, Kano visited many of the historical sites that he had read about in his studies of Chinese classics. While Kano was on his way back home, pirates surrounded his ship, but

Kano and his small group of Japanese remained unruffled and looked so menacing that the pirates backed off.

To be honest, however, Kano was appalled by the dirt, poverty, and backwardness of China. He wondered why Paris was so much better and more beautiful than Shanghai. Europeans seemed to be taking over the country economically with little resistance from the Chinese. He wondered how such a great civilization could have fallen so far. Kano felt that both the Chinese government and the nation's educational system were to blame. Just as Japanese students had gone abroad to learn in Europe and the United States during the Meiji period, Kano hoped that as many Chinese officials and exchange students as possible could study overseas, specifically in Japan, in order to get a fresh outlook on their own nation and China's role in international society. That is the reason the Kobun Gakuen was established.

Over the years, about eight thousand Chinese exchange students studied at Kobun Gakuen. The course of study was intended to be three years, with a curriculum of the usual courses in history, geography, science, mathematics, art, and so forth. Japanese and English were the language requirements, and physical education was necessary for both students and teachers. Here is an entry from a Chinese student's diary about his first impressions of the Kobun Gakuen.

The school is located far from the center of town. The scenery is nice, but the roads are terrible. The food at the school is meager. However, the classrooms, study halls, bathrooms, etc., are spotlessly clean, the exact opposite of China. Everything seems well organized. I noticed that the male students all had their hair cut short, so I cut mine too. The principal of the school is a gentleman called Jigoro Kano. He is said to be a famous educator. He guided us new students around the facilities, and later gave a speech at the formal entrance ceremony. He told us to study hard and work for the peace and prosperity of both our homeland and all of Asia. Classes in basic Japanese started the next day.

For a variety of reasons, not many of the Chinese students finished the three full years of study. It must be said that many of them spent more time engaging in radical activism than hitting the books. In fact, the Kobun Gakuen can be considered a kind of incubation tank for the Chinese Xinhai Revolution.

Kano gave three or four formal lectures a year to the student body of the Kobun Gakuen. He also kept in touch with many of his Chinese students; whenever he visited Shanghai, there was always a gathering of former Kobun Gakuen students. A dojo was built nearby, and Chinese students were encouraged to take up judo, although it was not a requirement. A few of them earned first dan during their stay in Tokyo. (Kobun Gakuen closed in 1909 due to a variety of factors, the main ones being fewer students because of the increasing turmoil in China, and less support from the Japanese government. However, a number of Chinese and a few Korean exchange students continued to study full-time at Kano's Tokyo Teacher Training College.)

Finally, in 1897, Kano's main job became serving as principal of Tokyo Teacher Training College, the pioneer educational institution for the new generation of teachers in Japan. Kano had a number of ideas that he espoused ceaselessly throughout his career, on how to organize the educational system in Japan based on conservative Confucian values combined with contemporary European liberal educational philosophy. Kano was interested in all aspects of education, from primary school to the college level. He was a "progressive" constantly at loggerheads with bureaucrats and political appointees at the Ministry of Education, especially those who wanted to turn the campus of the Tokyo Teacher Training College into a giant ROTC center for military activities. Nationalists viewed physical education as a means for training fit soldiers. Education must be pleasant, Kano insisted, beneficial for the student and beneficial for society, not a grim preparation to sacrifice one's life for the state in a war. The better the education a soldier receives, the better he will behave, not only as a serviceman but also as a citizen. Good education makes good thinkers with an international outlook, not ready to fight but willing to keep the peace.

Concurrent to Kano's efforts at promoting Kodokan judo was his drive to establish a required physical education program in every school in Japan. In the late nineteenth century, there was a worldwide craze for physical culture—calisthenics, gymnastics, yoga, track and field, and organized sports. Kano was an early convert to the cult of the body. While Kano devoted most of his time to the practice of jujutsu in his youth, he also enjoyed gymnastics and other newly introduced sports such as baseball, hiking, and rowing. Kano emphasized that exercise of the body was just as important as exercise of the mind for developing teachers. At Tokyo Teacher Training College, he established the following sports clubs: judo, kendo, sumo, gymnastics, tennis, baseball, and soccer. Students were required to pick one club and practice at least thirty minutes a day. Every student had to learn to swim. There was a huge school field day every year.

Kano wanted his graduates to push for physical education at their schools. In fact, he eventually saw the need for instructors who actually specialized in physical education. Kano established physical education as a major at his school. In 1908, the Japanese Diet passed a bill requiring all middle school students to be instructed in either kendo or judo. Further, Kano supported a national Japanese Association of Physical Education and served as the association's first president in 1909. Kano is considered the "Father of Physical Education in Japan." (Kano did not like the term *sport*, associating that word with "play." Kano insisted that what he wanted was physical education for the body and mind, not sports that created competition and rivalry.)

It was not only physical education that Kano promoted in his school. He was an avid supporter of the music department. After all, music was one of the six arts that Confucius recommended for a complete education. Kano—who enjoyed both Eastern and Western music—worked to get an independent School of Music established, and to make music education part of the curriculum at middle and high schools. In that regard, Kano can be considered the "Father of Musical Education in Japan."

A portrait of the dapper Kano in his vigorous fifties.

The ideal education was like that Kano himself had received, a harmonious blend of Eastern and Western learning. Kano stood his ground, like a good judo man, in his crusade for educational reform even though he was forced to resign his position as principal of Tokyo Teacher Training College twice—in 1897 and 1898. Kano was appointed principal for a third and final time in 1901, and stayed on until his retirement in 1921, all the while fighting, as best he could, for his principles.

Kano's View of Other Martial Arts and Masters of the Time

In 1906, the Butokukai, the national martial arts association, organized a conference among the various jujutsu schools in an attempt to establish parameters for modern jujutsu kata and set uniform rules for contests. Since Kano was in charge, the Kodokan had the most members on the committee (six out of twenty: Kano, Yokoyama, Yamashita, Isogai, Nagaoka, and Sato). Other schools represented were Takenouchi ryu (three members: Shikataro Takano, Kotaro Imai, and Hikosaburo Oshima); Yoshin ryu (three members: Eibi Totsuka, Takayoshi Katayama, and Katsuta Hiratsuka); Sekiguchi ryu (two members: Jushin Sekiguchi and Mokichi Tsumizu); and, with one member each, the Takeuchi Santo ryu (Koji Yano), Fusen ryu (Mataemon Tanabe), Shiten ryu (Kumon Hoshino), Miura ryu (Masamizu Inazu), Kyushin ryu (Yazo Eguchi), and Sosuishitsu ryu (Kihei Aoyanagi). The new guidelines essentially followed the Kodokan approach. However, nothing concrete came from this and other conclaves. Every ryu continued to pretty much do its own thing.

What was Kano's relationship with other martial arts masters besides those of jujutsu?

The three most popular martial arts in Kano's time were kendo, judo, and sumo. While Kano was keen on having his judo students learn from other martial art traditions, he was much less enthusiastic about them practicing modern kendo. Kano himself evidently never practiced kendo at all, and showed little interest in swordsmanship or other weapons systems historically or technically, although later he did sponsor a Traditional Bujutsu Research Group at the Kodokan that conducted research on bojutsu, kenjutsu, and *jodo* (stick fighting). Kano knew the swordsman Yamaoka Tesshu (1836–88). Tesshu was one of the best-known martial artists in Japan, founder of the Muto (No Sword) ryu school of swordsmanship, adviser to the Emperor Meiji, lay Zen master, and famous calligrapher. Since Tesshu brushed the calligraphic inscription engraved on Kano's father's gravestone, Kano must

Kano and his disciples who attended the Butokukai conclave of jujutsu instructors in Kyoto, on July 24, 1906. *First row from left:* Yoshitsugu Yamashita, Jigoro Kano, and Sakujiro Yokoyama; *second row:* Hoken Sato, Hajime Isogai, and Shuichi Nagaoka.

have respected Tesshu highly. Nonetheless, Kano never refers to Tesshu in his writings or lectures—perhaps because down-to-earth Kano was on a judo quest with little interest in swordsmanship or Zen enlightenment. (The superefficient and ever-active Kano likely considered sitting still for thirty minutes in meditation a complete waste of time.)

In principle, Kano wrote that kendo kata could be integrated into judo kata, but in fact, he had a low opinion of modern kendo—ironically, for the same reasons that were initially given to him about jujutsu: the art is no longer relevant in modern society;

"Who walks around with a sword?" Also, he considered kendo too one-dimensional. Unlike judo, which provided thorough physical education for the entire body, kendo practitioners had limited options on how to move the body and feet. Not to mention that kendo people are in fact training to symbolically "kill" their opponents rather than throwing them safely to a padded mat. In addition, kendo practice involved a lot of expensive equipment that was burdensome to haul around, unlike a light, compact judo uniform that could be carried anywhere in a small bundle. Kano wrote about judo and kendo people working together to develop a system of mutual training, but it doesn't seem possible to cross-train if one side is armed and in armor and one side is not. It is clear that Kano believed that in any exchange, the kendo people would benefit much more from the judo people than the other way around. Kano believed that judo was the best choice as a martial art for both modern Japanese and interested members of the world community.

Nonetheless, Kano always supported the practice of kendo in schools, and had an active kendo physical education program at the Tokyo Teacher Training College. Kano employed one of Tesshu's top disciples, Sasaburo Takano (1862–1950), as a kendo instructor at the school. Kano frequently met with Hakudo Nakayama (1872–1958), perhaps the premier swordsman of the day, to discuss the issues related to the practice of judo and kendo in modern society. Since many judo people did kendo concurrently, achieving high ranks in both disciplines, it shows that the two systems can be companionable.

Kano liked sumo. It had much more connection to judo. Sumo has simple rules, the opponents have to remain standing (so there was none of the groundwork Kano disliked), hardly any clothing is necessary, the match is easily decided, and it can be practiced outdoors in the fresh air. Many judo throws are based on sumo techniques. Not a few professional sumo wrestlers got their start in judo because it was an easy transition. Kano got sumo included as a possible elective for physical education in Japanese schools, and he encouraged the wide practice of amateur sumo.

In 1925, Kano had the opportunity to see Okinawan karate

Jigoro Kano shaking hands with the kendo master Sasaburo Takano, an instructor at the Tokyo Teacher Training College.

master Gichin Funakoshi (1868–1957) give a demonstration at the National Athletic Exhibition sponsored by the Japanese Ministry of Education in Tokyo. Kano was impressed, and he asked Funakoshi to teach a few suitable kata at the Kodokan. In fact, Kano had corresponded with Funakoshi several years earlier about the possibility of Funakoshi coming to teach at the Kodokan, but at that time Funakoshi declined, saying, "I'm still in the process of learning karate myself."

This time, Funakoshi accepted the invitation. At first, Funakoshi was awed by the intensity, size, and high quality of the Kodokan trainees—there was nothing like that in Okinawa. Nevertheless, Funakoshi's lessons were well received. Kano adopted certain karate movements that Funakoshi demonstrated into judo kata, and asked Funakoshi to head up a Kodokan "Karate Division." Funakoshi politely declined, fearing that his karate system

Kano (right) demonstrating atemi at a seminar held in Kobe in 1926.

would be swallowed up by the huge Kodokan organization. Nevertheless, Funakoshi was eternally grateful for Kano's kind initial support, and after the judo master's death in 1938, Funakoshi would bow in the direction of Kano's office whenever he passed by the Kodokan on the streetcar or in an automobile.

In 1927, Kano had a chance to visit Okinawa himself. There he witnessed a demonstration by Chojun Miyagi (1888–1953). Miyagi was doing for karate what Kano did for judo: adopting and arranging various fighting arts—some traditional Okinawan, some Chinese based—into a coherent system (later known as Goju ryu karate). Miyagi did not just punch and kick. There were throws, pins, joint locks, and groundwork in his demonstration. (An added feature was Miyagi tearing the bark off a tree and ripping pieces of meat apart with his bare hands.) Like Kano, Miyagi developed his system after extensive research and taught it in a logical manner, with reference to physical and medical sciences.

Kano was impressed, so he arranged for Miyagi to give demonstrations on the Japanese mainland. Miyagi went on to become a central figure in the establishment of karate as a distinct and important martial art recognized by the Butokukai.

Incidentally, while he was in Okinawa, Kano witnessed a battle between a mongoose and a deadly poisonous adder. (Such battles were, and still are, staged for tourists.) As is usually the case, the mongoose killed the adder because, as Kano observed, the animal practiced judo: "It dodged the adder's strikes and immediately counterattacked with perfect timing."

Similarly, Kano was asked how a judo man would handle himself against a bigger wild animal such as a bear. He replied, "Bears are ferocious when cornered, but they will shy away from loud noises or bright lights. The best kind of judo is to keep the bear at bay with proper precautions rather than attempt to confront it face-to-face."

In October 1930, after hearing much about Morihei Ueshiba (1883–1969) from his students, Kano paid a visit to Ueshiba's temporary dojo in Meijiro. Like everyone else, he was dazzled by Ueshiba's seemingly superhuman demonstration. He said of Ueshiba's performance: "This is ideal budo; it is true judo." (A Kodokan instructor named Nagaoka who was present joked, "Does the mean we are learning fake judo?") Later, after the demonstration, Kano sent Ueshiba a letter of appreciation and asked him to teach several advanced students from the Kodokan.

A number of Kodokan judo men trained simultaneously under Ueshiba, most notably Kenji Tomita, who had been Kano's and Ueshiba's student since 1906, and Minoru Mochizuki, who was sent to train with Ueshiba after the demonstration in 1930. A couple of Kodokan men even switched entirely to Ueshiba ryu jujutsu, later to become aikido. One rather rude and ungrateful fellow, a Kodokan sixth dan named Tetsuo Hoshi (d. 1947), actually returned his rank to the Kodokan after being tossed about by Ueshiba. (Hoshi was later executed as a World War II war criminal for torturing prisoners of war with his martial art techniques.)

Another influential (and dreaded) martial artist of day was Sokaku Takeda (1859–1943). Kano and Sokaku were total opposites. While Kano graduated from Tokyo University, Sokaku never learned to read or write because of his chaotic upbringing. Kano fought in contests with clearly defined rules, man-to-man unarmed combat, and was proud of the fact that he had never injured an opponent seriously. Sokaku, on the other hand, engaged in scores of fights to the finish—in self-defense, in response to challenges, and while teaching—with all manner of weapons (including a wet towel), killing or maiming dozens. When Sokaku saw another human being, he saw an enemy; Kano saw a potential convert to the Way of Judo. Kano devoted his life to building the Kodokan literally and figuratively in the heart of Tokyo. Sokaku spent his entire life wandering, usually in the remotest parts of Japan, frequently disappearing for long periods of time. Kano and Sokaku certainly met, and some of the Kodokan people trained under the Daito ryu master. Sokaku was known to be highly critical of Kodokan judo—"Worthless, not budo, too much like a dance"—but Sokaku's son Tokimune stated that Kano and Sokaku were on good terms personally, and that Sokaku would visit Kano when he was in Tokyo. There seems to be no mention of Sokaku or the Daito ryu in Kano's writings, but Kano was not interested in incorporating devastating body and weapons techniques into Kodokan judo, and the worldviews of Kano and Sokaku were not compatible.

Kano as a Cultural and Political Force

Since Kano was a professional educator, constantly giving lectures, it is natural that he wanted them collected and published together with articles of interest by other thinkers. From 1898, beginning with the magazine *Kokushi* (Patriot), Kano published a series of different journals: *Judo, Yuko no Katsudo* (Effective Living), *Ozei* (The Majority), *Judokai* (Judo World), *Sakko* (Awakening), and finally a newer version of *Judo*. These publications contained articles regarding the important social issues of the day, the development of a Japanese national cultural identity, educational policy, local and international politics, judo philosophy and technique, Kano's travelogues, reports on the Olympic movement, plus a question-and-answer column by Kano himself.

In order to disseminate his ideas on judo, modern education, and social issues, in March 1922, Kano established the Kodokan Culture Council. The council's lofty aims:

> To promote the ideas of *seiryoku saizen katsu*, "Effective use of focused effort, maximum efficiency." This principle can be applied to all aspects of one's life.
>
> 1. To seek perfection of each individual, physically, intellectually, and morally, in order for him or her to be capable of benefiting society.
> 2. To honor the history and culture of Japan and work to improve whatever is beneficial for the nation.
> 3. To promote social cohesion through mutual cooperation between individuals as well as between organizations.
> 4. To seek to eliminate racial prejudice and promote human rights worldwide through peaceful means and international cooperation.

General Principles

1. Perfection of oneself is the best use of one's energies.
2. Self-perfection leads to success in one's endeavors.
3. The perfection of oneself together with others is the basis of human welfare.

These were the principles that guided Kano himself throughout his public and private life.

The Kodokan had many distinguished foreign visitors over the years. One was John Dewey, the American philosopher whose progressive ideas on education appealed to Kano. Dewey paid a visit to the Kodokan on March 31, 1919. Here is an excerpt from his diary *Letters from China and Japan* describing his visit:

The great judo expert [Kano] is president of a normal school, and he arranged a special demonstration by experts for my benefit, he explaining the theory of each part of it in advance. It took place Sunday morning in a big Judo hall [Kodokan], and there were lots of couples doing "free" work, too; they are too quick for my eye in that to see anything but persons suddenly thrown over somebody's back and flopped down on the ground. It is really an art. The Professor took the old practices and studied them, worked out their mechanical principles, and then devised a graded scientific set of exercises. The system is really not a lot of tricks, but is based on the elementary laws of mechanics, a study of the equilibrium of the human body, the ways in which it is disturbed, how to recover your own and take advantage of the shifting of the center of gravity of the other person. The first thing that is taught is how to fall down without being hurt, that alone is worth the price of admission and ought to be taught in all our gyms. It isn't a good substitute for out-of-door games, but I think much better than most of our inside formal gymnastics. The mental element is much stronger. In short, I think, a study ought to be made from the standpoint of conscious control. . . . I noticed in the Judo the small waists of all these people; they breathe always from the abdomen. Their biceps are not especially large, but their forearms are larger than any I have ever seen. I have yet to see a Japanese throw back his head when he rises. In the army they have an indirect method of deep breathing which really goes back to the Buddhist Zen teaching of the old Samurai.

(It is interesting to note Dewey's reference to Zen; Kano would never have used the concept of Zen to describe his philosophy of Kodokan judo.)

Although he did not visit the Kodokan proper, in 1924, Edward, Prince of Wales, witnessed a demonstration of judo staged for him at the Seinenkan Hall on the imperial grounds. The diminutive Kyuzo Mifune threw ten opponents—all third or fourth dan, selected for their large size—in a row, employing various throws and pins, including his trademark "air throw" (*kuki-nage*). The prince was impressed.

In 1929, the Indian philosopher and Nobel Prize winner Rabindranath Tagore (1861–1941), visited the Kodokan. For nearly twenty years, Jinnotsuke Sano had been teaching basic judo at Tagore's Shantinikan academy but had departed. Tagore wanted to revive judo practice at the academy, and it was arranged for Shinzo Takagaki (1893–1977) to go to India. Takagaki stayed for two years, teaching and demonstrating judo all over India. One revolutionary practice introduced at the Shantinikan dojo was that girls and boys trained together, something unheard of in India at the time.

Political Career

As mentioned, in 1922 Kano became a member of the House of Peers, the upper house of the Japanese Diet, nominated by the Privy Council at the recommendation of his colleague Prime Minister Korekiyo Takahashi (1854–1936). He told Kano, "We need people who think like you do on the inside, not the outside, of government."

(Takahashi was another amazing "Meiji man." As a young man, he was sent overseas to study even before the Meiji Restoration of 1868. He worked as houseboy in England and then a farmhand in Oakland, California, where he participated in labor strikes. Following his return to Japan, Takahashi went broke during a period of dissipation. After these experiences, Takahashi understood the value of money. Takahashi turned Christian. He eventually became Japan's wizard of finance, serving as governor of the Bank of Japan and then longtime finance minister. He was prime minister for seven months [November 13, 1921, through June 12, 1922] but was better at being finance minister and returned to that post in successive cabinets. Takahashi's financial policies infuriated the military, and he was assassinated by rebel military officers in 1936 during the February 26 incident. Because Takahashi had a full beard, a stout build, and a meditative demeanor, he was known as "Finance Minister Daruma." In 1951, Takahashi's smiling Daruma face was displayed on a fifty-yen note.)

The House of Peers was comprised of aristocrats, high-ranking members of society, and wealthy taxpayers. Some of the members were elected, but most were appointed for life from the aristocracy. A few nonaristocrats, such as Kano, received special election. Kano did not join any political faction and remained a backbencher, doing what he was always doing, promoting Kodokan judo and working with—or sometimes against—the Ministry of Education. Thus, Kano's tenure as a member of the House of Peers was spent mostly behind the scenes; he seems not to have played much of an active role in the politics of the place. Actually, he was not very popular in the House. Other members, many with aristocratic titles, were irked that nonaristocrat Kano did not show them the customary deference when he met them. As a head of the Kodokan and principal of the nation's top Teacher Training College, Kano was used to being in charge. He respected people for what they had accomplished, not what they said. There was even a rumor that Kano planned to form a Kodokan political party that would field members to run in elections. (In fact, a number of Kodokan members were elected on their own to various offices, including prime minister, across the country. However, the Kodokan members were of too broad a spectrum to form a unified political front.)

In the 1920s and 1930s, Kano was in a very difficult situation politically. The policies of the Japanese government became more and more extreme. One example: for decades Kano resisted supporting the Imperial Rescript on Education promulgated in 1890. The rescript essentially demanded worship of the emperor as a Shinto deity. Kano was totally secular in outlook, and rational in thought. He was a Confucian through and through, with little interest in any nebulous religious or mystical mumbo jumbo, especially that the emperor was somehow "divine." Kano believed that the emphasis on one religion in the rescript would make followers of other religions (or no religion) ignore it.

Unfortunately, copies of the rescript had been sent to all schools, together with a portrait of the emperor, with directions to pay homage to the portrait every day before class. Graduates from his college were employed as schoolteachers everywhere, and Kano could not instruct them to refuse to bow to the emperor's photo. Teachers had to go along, whether they liked it or not; otherwise, they would have been dismissed (or worse). Although Kano clearly didn't like the rescript—it was contrary to all his ideas on what modern education should be—he finally felt compelled, in 1922, thirty years after the rescript had been promulgated, to support national recognition of the rescript as a moral code, not a religious doctrine. To the last, Kano resisted having to enshrine a *shinden* (*kamidama*), a Shinto altar dedicated to Amaterasu (the emperor was supposed to be a direct descendant), at the Kodokan until forced to do so under government pressure in 1937.

In principle, Kano was in favor of the imperial family, believing that the emperor could serve as a unifying force above the partisan political fray. He gave instruction to Emperor Taisho when Taisho was a student at the Peers School, and he lectured formally to Hirohito at the palace. Kano evidently had several private meetings with Hirohito, too. Kano may well have had some influence with the emperor (but not enough).

Right-wingers and ultranationalists surrounded Kano. Kano must have had some dealings with the ultraright kingpin Mitsuru Toyama (1855–1944)—everybody did. Nicknamed the "Shadow Shogun" and the "Boss of Bosses," Toyama was the most powerful private citizen in Japan at the time. Toyama was involved in every type of major political and economic activity of the country, primarily through the auspices of the Genyosha, a secret society and terrorist organization that he founded in 1881. It is not clear how much Kano had to deal with Toyama, but many of Kano's Kodokan senior students were disciples of Toyama, and one of them (Ryohei Uchida) actually founded the Black Dragon Society under Toyama's direction. In some ways, Toyama was a fascist thug; in other ways, he was a "Zen gangster," selfless, austere, and working quietly behind the scenes for what he considered to be best for his country and Asia at large.

Kano was a member of the Kinyo-kai (the Friday Club), established by Kiichiro Hiranuma (1867–1952) and Somei Uzawa (1872–1955), two other powerful right-wingers. Like every major figure of the times, Hiranuma was a complex character. As a prosecutor at the Ministry of Justice, Hiranuma went after corruption in the government and political parties, winning numerous convictions. He served as chief justice of the Supreme Court, justice minister, prime minister (in 1939), home minister, and as a *jushin* (unofficial adviser to Hirohito during the war). He was as extreme as an extremist can be, promoting worship of the emperor, imperialist expansionism, suppression of human rights, and violent repression of opponents of the government. Hiranuma was the one who issued the arrest order for Morihei Ueshiba during the crackdown on the Omoto-kyo religious sect for lèse-majesté in 1935. Not surprisingly, Hiranuma was arrested as a class A war criminal following the end of the war. The chief defense lawyer who represented Hiranuma during his trial at the tribunal was Somei Uzawa. Uzawa had been involved in many high-profile cases over the years, and also acted as the Kodokan's lawyer.

Kano gave several lectures at the Friday Club, but they were hardly right-wing harangues against Japan's perceived internal and external enemies. Kano's lectures were on how to solve international conflict through judo principles, the importance of modern education (again based on judo principles), and his favorite theme, "Mutual Well-being and Prosperity through Application of Focused Effort, Maximum Efficiency." Kano even demonstrated judo on some of the members at the club. They were amazed at how gentle judo appeared.

Kano was obliged to compromise on certain policies he disagreed with in order to advance his own cause in other ways. In other words, he stayed in the middle, adhering to a key judo concept. Kano's political views and actions were similar to those of Kinmochi Saionji (1849–1940), who served as prime minister from 1906 to 1908.

Saionji and Kano had parallel careers and were alike in many ways. Saionji spent years overseas, traveling and studying law in France. He absorbed the ideals of liberty and fraternity prevalent in that country. Through his travels in the United States and Europe, Saionji developed an international and informed outlook. Back in Japan, Saionji served as minister of education in several cabinets, and worked with Kano on the modernization of Japan's educational system along progressive lines. As prime minster, liberal Saionji defended a democratic, constitutional form of government against the demands of reactionary politicians and the military. Saionji never stopped opposing the militarists, and in 1936 he was the target of an assassination attempt. Both Saionji and Kano had devoted their lives to international understanding and cooperation, and were quite aware that narrow nationalism and military confrontation—for Japan or any other country, for that matter—is not the way to proceed. As Kano often taught, "No one wins in a war." Saionji's critics branded him a "globalist"—a description that aptly fits Kano as well—as if that were the worst sin possible for a Japanese politician.

Saionji and Kano were certainly patriots but not nationalists. Both were aware of the great benefits Japan had received from opening the country to the world. Both believed that Japan could learn many things from the West; also that there were many things the West could learn from Japan (one of those things being judo). Nonetheless, like all of us everywhere, Saionji and Kano had to compromise politically and socially. It could not be helped. Furthermore, it is unfair to Kano and Saionji to accuse them of "guilt by association," or judge them by impossibly high standards, ignoring the realities and complexities of the situation— that is, to blame them for being Japanese at that time in history.

Kano's Olympic Dream

In 1909, Japan was invited to the 1912 Olympics. At a loss for how to respond to the invitation, not surprisingly, the Japanese government turned to Kano, who was an expert in physical education

Kano at the time of his election to the International Olympic Committee.

and experienced in international affairs. After some study of the matter, Kano agreed to represent Japan. The Japanese government submitted Kano's name to the International Olympic Committee (IOC), and he was duly elected its first Asian member. He was the official representative of Japan in the 1912 Olympics in Stockholm. The Japanese contingent consisted of only two track-and-field runners, but at least the nation established a presence.

On his way back from the Stockholm Olympics, Kano visited the United States for the first time, stopping briefly in New York, where he delivered a lecture and demonstration. Kano also stopped in the Territory of Hawaii and visited the Honolulu dojo that had been opened in 1909. Kano was to visit the United States two more times, in 1920 and 1938. Each time he was there, Kano exhorted *nikei-jin* (those of Japanese ancestry) to become "patriotic American citizens."

Kano led the Japanese delegation to the 1920 Antwerp Olympics. This time Japan was able to field a team of over a hundred, consisting of athletes, coaches, and officials. Japan had two bronze medal winners—in tennis, of all things. Kano skipped the 1924 Olympics in Paris and attended the 1928 Olympics in Amsterdam, but as a private citizen. During those years, there was a lot of political turmoil in Japan regarding how to participate in the games and at what cost; Kano was evidently on the outs with the various organizations involved.

However, in 1931, the Tokyo City Council decided to make a serious pitch for the 1940 Olympics. As is the case for every Olympics, there are questions of a sponsoring city having adequate athletic facilities, public transportation, sufficient lodging for visitors, and, most important, enough of a budget. Tokyo seemed to be seriously deficient in all these requirements, not to mention that it was located in the Far East, so its bid seemed like a long shot. Due to his international reputation and experience, Kano was really the only hope as Tokyo's spokesman.

Fortunately, Kano relished the challenge of presenting Tokyo's case, and he devoted himself wholeheartedly to the cause, especially since the odds were so much against him. Kano grew up in the Meiji period, during which the motto of the time was, "Unified in body and mind, there is nothing a human being cannot accomplish!"

After the new four-story Kodokan opened in Suidobashi in 1934, Kano spent nearly all his time, at home and abroad, promoting Tokyo's bid for the 1940 Olympics. There were many obstacles: possible bids by other cities (Rome, Helsinki, and London); international politics; economic considerations resulting in commercialization of the games; backroom machinations by politicians, businessmen, and the military; Tokyo's distant location; bribery of officials; racism; and, not least of all, opposition to the bid in Japan itself. (Of course, such shenanigans plague every Olympic bid, past, present, or future.)

The 1932 Olympics were held in Los Angeles. Kano spent the days before and after ceaselessly politicking for Tokyo's bid all over the United States. He did the same in Europe later, between

1934 and the 1936 Berlin Olympics, meeting with top officials in nearly every European country.

The major stumbling block to a successful bid by Tokyo was the war Japan instigated in China in 1937. The issue was immediately raised: "How can a nation at war hold an Olympics, an event that is intended to promote peace?" Rather than risk losing everything, Kano lamely made excuses for his country: "War in China has nothing to do with sports." "Japan's real intentions in China are to make it a better country by ridding it of factionalism." "As long as Chinese warplanes do not bomb Tokyo, there is nothing to worry about."

Kano deftly addressed all the arguments—political, economic, and organizational—against Japan, and after much behind-the-scenes drama and horse trading, Kano's efforts were rewarded at the 1938 IOC meeting in Cairo. Kano said of the meeting, "My opponents attempted to swamp me and drown me out, but I would not be deterred." The committee confirmed Tokyo as the site of the 1940 Olympics.

Kano vowed that Japan would not turn the Olympics into a nationalist spectacle like the 1936 Berlin games. It would be a true Olympics, bringing nations together in a spirit of peace and friendship.

Interestingly, Kano did not lobby for judo to be included in the 1940 Tokyo games. On the contrary, he was reluctant to have judo put on the program because "judo is not a sport. It is an art. It is a science. It is a way of life." Kano believed that inclusion of judo in the Olympics would alter its character as a vehicle to bring people together. National judo organizations would fiercely compete among themselves to win a medal "at any cost and by any means." That is not the purpose of judo. Kano was open to the idea of judo's inclusion in the games if other countries were in favor, but he did not push it. For Kano, the Olympics were all about fair play. When European delegates proposed to hold the games in August, Kano suggested September instead: "The weather in Japan in August is very hot and humid. Japanese competitors, who are accustomed to such muggy conditions, would have a decided advantage over athletes from other countries."

Kano on the deck of the *Hikawa-maru*. The photo was taken a few days before his death.

Even though Tokyo's bid seemed secure, Kano sensed that Japan's increasing militarization and warmongering would destroy all his efforts. On his trip back home from Cairo via Vancouver on the ship *Hikawa-maru*, it was clear that Kano was exhausted, physically and mentally. While he should have been elated by his success in Cairo, he looked disappointed, almost distraught.

Kano was obsessed with getting the 1940 Olympics held in Tokyo—at any cost. Against his doctor's orders, Kano insisted on making the arduous trip to Cairo in 1938. He refused to take anyone to accompany him; "they would just get in the way." The last thing Kano wrote before his departure was a farewell letter to wife. In my opinion, getting the Olympic Games for Tokyo was Kano's way of waging peace. If the Olympics were to come to

Memorial photograph of Kano displayed at his funeral.

Tokyo, the Japanese military would have to behave itself. If other countries had to field an Olympic team, there would be less time and money to field an army. For the games to be held in 1940, there needed to be an informal truce among nations until then and with hope for its continuation thereafter.

The *Hikawa-maru* set sail for Japan on April 22, 1938. At the beginning of May, Kano become quite ill; I feel it was a case of "I am sick because the world is sick." He continued to try to eat food and drink sake each day but gradually became weaker and weaker. Kano died early on the morning of May 4, 1938, at age seventy-seven. The cause of death is recorded as pneumonia. There was not a single Kodokan member on the ship.

Upon the *Hikawa-maru's* return to Japan, Kano's coffin was draped with the Olympic flag and lowered from the ship. On May

9, Kano was given a Shinto funeral at the Kodokan, with thousands of mourners in attendance.

Sadly, within two months of Kano's death, the 1940 Tokyo Olympics were canceled as "being a distraction to the national interests of Japan." War had started in Asia and was about to break out in Europe and the Pacific. After Kano's death, judo was presented at the Kodokan as a "manifestation of the unique Japanese spirit." Judo became another weapon in the nation's arsenal. A bronze image of Kano that had been erected in front of the Tokyo Teacher Training College was melted down in 1939 to help with the war effort.

Given his peripatetic lifestyle, it is not surprising that Kano died on a journey. He was always on the move, seeking better, more efficient, and beneficial means of presenting his message. And Kano's life was not in vain. In 1958, the statue of Kano was recast. One image was replaced in front of the college (now the University of Tsukuba) and one was placed in the entrance of the Kodokan. His life and message continues to inspire people all over the world. As he believed, "The teaching of one virtuous person can influence many; that which has been learned well in one generation can be passed on to a hundred."

2

Kano, the Man Himself

◉

KANO WAS THE MOST PUBLIC of public figures. He was always out in the world—directing the Kodokan, teaching and lecturing in all kinds of educational institutions, traveling the globe at the request of the Ministry of Education, and promoting the cause of the Olympic Games. It seems that he hardly had any time for a private life. Here is a glimpse of Kano, the man himself.

Kano's Family Life

Regarding his family, it was "like father, like son." Kano's children remember him as mostly absent. When he was home, he spent much of his time in his study; in fact, after his family lined up at the entranceway to welcome Kano home, that is where he went immediately.

Kano seems to have taught his wife, Sumako, a little judo, beginning on their honeymoon, but her training could not continue long, as Kano and Sumako went on to have eight children, five daughters and three sons. As is often the case with children of famous parents, a couple of the Kano kids turned resentful and rebellious. None of the Kano sons practiced judo, and two of them seem to have hated it.

The first son, Rishin (1897–1934), was a painter. He studied art in Europe, and took the drastic step of giving up the Kano name, taking his mother's family name instead, becoming Rishin

The Kano family circa 1902, with six of their eight children. Risei, the second son and third director of the Kodokan, is second from the right.

Takezoe. Kano did not shed a tear when Rishin died, and went to work as usual the day after his son's death. The second son, Risei (1901–86), worked for the imperial household as keeper of the archives. He became the third president of the Kodokan in 1946, after president number two, Jiro Nango, who was Kano's nephew and a student at both Kano's private academy and the Kodokan. Since Nango was a vice admiral in the Imperial Navy, Occupation authorities deemed him unacceptable to head anything, so he had to be removed from his Kodokan post. Although Risei Kano replaced Nango reluctantly, it must be said that he served as head of the Kodokan from 1946 to 1980, the period of the Kodokan's worldwide expansion (albeit as a sport, not as a way of life as his father had intended).

The third son, Riho (1912–46), was the black sheep of the family. Arrested twice by the military police for "consorting with communists," Riho had decidedly left-wing views. Kano had to interrupt an important European trip to get Riho released from prison. Kano was severely criticized for Riho's behavior, to the extent that two of the senior instructors at the Kodokan demanded his resignation. If Kano did not resign, they threatened to bolt and establish their own judo organization. Disappointingly, Kano did not stand up for his son Riho, and only made excuses. "Riho was not raised like that. He has been living away from home for a long time. I was in Europe when he was fired from his teaching job in Shizuoka, and I could not counsel him." Kano was able to get Riho released from jail but immediately sent him to the United States to study at the University of Chicago. Riho remained committed to left-wing causes and worked as a foreign correspondent for the Japanese newspaper *Asahi Shimbun*. He died in an automobile accident in 1946.

The Kano daughters too practiced little judo, although the first daughter, Noriko (1893–1956), was director of the Women's Division of the Kodokan when it was founded in 1926 and was eventually awarded first dan. Noriko married Tetsuo Watanuki, a respected professor of literature. Noriko seems to have been Kano's favorite child. Even Noriko, however, reminisced that it was not until he was in his seventies that Kano began acting as a father and grandfather. Kano would play with the grandkids, and take his family on excursions, often to visit his daughters in different parts of Japan.

Daughters Tadako (b. 1895) and Sawako (b. 1898) were wed to the same man, Kazu Shogenji, one of Kano's paternal relatives. Sawako Kano became Shogenji's second wife after his first wife, Tadako Kano, died. Mareko (b. 1899–1959) married businessman Kojiro Hatanaka. Atsuko (b. 1907) married a judo man, Masami Takasaki, introduced to her by her father. Takasaki, winner of the first All-Japan Judo Championship Tournament in 1930, eventually attained ninth dan. (The year of death for Tadako, Sawako, and Atsuko is unknown.)

While Kano's children did not care much for judo, many of his nephews and nieces studied under their uncle at his private academy, the Kodokan, or at one of the schools where he was principal.

(Kano's grandson Yukimitsu, son of Risei, was the fourth president of the Kodokan, from 1980 to 2009. Yukimitsu practiced some judo, obtaining first dan. The current head of the Kodokan is Haruki Uemura, world champion in the heavyweight division at the 1976 Olympics. Yukimitsu Kano's two daughters have "nothing to do with judo." It is unlikely that the Kodokan will ever again be headed by a member of the Kano family. That may have been the way Kano intended it to be all along. Kano was naturally concerned about the future of the Kodokan after his death but, for various reasons, did not want his family involved in the succession. Kano favored the establishment of an executive board with the power to run the Kodokan after his passing. However, in the final years of his life, Kano was literally consumed by his drive to have the 1940 Olympics held in Tokyo. Since he died unexpectedly in 1938, nothing was settled.)

The Kano family lived simply, frugal in their habits, never spending money on fine clothes or accessories, or expensive meals. That was the samurai way of living: unostentatious, nothing extravagant or gaudy, austere and dignified. Kano also had a samurai's disdain for acquiring money and for bookkeeping; as we shall see, that noble but impractical attitude in the modern age nearly bankrupted him.

Personality and Habits

In his personal life, Kano followed his maxim "Focused effort, maximum efficiency." He hated wasting time. If anyone was late for an appointment with Kano, as soon as the person arrived, he announced, "Meeting is over. Get out."

He was not interested in dealing with trifling details. He ate the same thing every day for lunch so he wouldn't be bothered by having to decide what to order. He always carried an umbrella so he wouldn't be troubled about whether or not to take one with him. If he happened to be traveling with his children or grandchildren and they were waiting for a train or whatever, Kano would ask them to try to name the objects around them in English so as not to waste an opportunity to study. When he went hiking in the mountains with his students, it was never simply to enjoy the sights. He told them, "As you walk along the trail, consider these important factors and how you would react: 'What if I got lost? What if I got caught in a thunderstorm, a flash flood, or a blizzard? What would I do if I got attacked by a wild animal?'" A trip to the beach was not meant to be just a pleasant excursion. It was an outdoor laboratory in which to learn not to be afraid of water and how to swim, especially important for every Japanese, whose nation is surrounded by the ocean.

Kano always got to the station just in time to catch the train to work, trying to take care of as many errands as he could along the way from home. On other occasions during longer trips that required transfers, Kano would spend two hours talking in a coffeehouse with colleagues if he deemed the subject important. Consequently, he would miss his train. On busy days such as during summer vacation, there were no first-class seats on the next train, so the principal of Tokyo Teacher Training College and president of the Kodokan went third class. The other third-class passengers were often either his school students or Kodokan members: "Look how frugal Kano Sensei is, traveling with us on third class." Kano himself was fine in either class, "as long as I get to my destination." Kano said this because he sometimes boarded the wrong train at a busy station due to his last-minute arrival at a platform.

Actually, traveling was the one occasion that Kano got to relax. He crammed every minute leading up to a trip with business, but as soon as he boarded the train, boat, or plane, Kano took it easy. Kano saw travel not as a tiring burden but as a refreshing break. When it was possible to fly on commercial airlines, Kano enjoyed traveling much more. "I love to soar among the clouds and look down on the continents and vast seas."

Kano believed that the practice of judo taught him how to be even tempered, never getting agitated or excited, displaying neither excessive joy nor extreme unhappiness, and accepting and dealing with things just as they are, just as they happen. During a drive from France to Italy, the car in which Kano was riding nearly ran off a cliff. Although the car was hanging halfway out over the valley, Kano, unruffled, told the other terrified passengers, "Don't worry. It will be all right. Someone will be here soon to rescue us."

Kano was a talker. Not small talk, but wide-ranging discussions, from the finer points to the broader implications of a subject. Unlike most Japanese, who tend to be shy and find it hard to express their opinions clearly, Kano was a good debater, both in his native tongue and in English. He never got angry or strident in his arguments—he used verbal judo. But he was tenacious. Kano refused to give in if he thought he was right, arguing, if necessary until midnight, with a guest at home or with officials (including the minister himself) at the Ministry of Education.

He wasn't much of a classroom lecturer, however. Students claimed his lectures were boring—although students say that about most of their teachers. On occasion, only two or three students would show up, infuriating Kano. In truth, he was a better administrator than classroom teacher. Kano did, however, make it a point to talk individually in the principal's office with every student at least once before he or she graduated. He always told his pupils, "Study is beautiful. When you study, be sure to dress properly, sit up straight, and treat your books, paper, and writing tools with respect."

Kano's five pieces of advice to his graduating students:

1. Do not drink too much.
2. Do not let your students see you going to the toilet. (This strange admonition, I presume, can be interpreted as "Always maintain your dignity in school, and do not let your private matters intrude on your public behavior.")
3. Never let anything shake your confidence.
4. Do not forget to apply the spirit of education in the broadest possible sense.
5. Even though you are graduating from teachers' college, it does not mean you have to become a teacher. You should be able to use the talents you have acquired in this college in any endeavor.

Here are a few examples of Kano's approach as an educator.
Kano told his students to "Keep moving, sleep well, study hard, enjoy completely." He also told them that "Differences of opinion are fine, indeed necessary; in the end, however, consensus is essential."

If Kano saw a student walking down the hall that looked pasty, Kano would stop him and say, "You need more exercise. Get some physical education." Kano said the same thing to any of his teachers that looked peaked when he met them in his office, or even during a meeting.

The college had a boat that was used for school events. When it was no longer functional, the students demanded that the school build a new one. Principal Kano refused because there was no extra money in the budget for that. He told them, "If you want a new boat, raise the money yourselves." The students did so, getting enough funds by gathering donations among themselves, teachers, and alumni. Kano did not contribute a yen, but when a new boat was built, he gave a large donation for the boat's maintenance. He told Ueno, the student leader of the fund-raising effort, "You have done a good job, almost too good. Activities such as this will not always be successful. If you lack support, there will be times when even the greatest individual effort will not be enough to accomplish a goal. Keep that in mind, and in life you will pick and choose your battles wisely."

As a principal, Kano was good at giving speeches at school ceremonies and other events, but even he admitted that they were frequently too long. Once at a lecture and public demonstration on judo he was giving to a general audience, Kano went on and on, holding up the judo practiced by women to be the ideal. He said the best judo was like a subtle martial arts dance, perfectly executed and beautiful to watch. Someone from the audience shouted, "Enough already! We came here to see a fight, not a dance! Show us a contest!" Kano said, "You can go anywhere to see a fight. I want to show you how to win without fighting!" Kano then got up and left.

Kano never missed a scheduled lecture even if he had to be carried to the forum on a stretcher.

Kano at age sixty-eight.

Kano kept diaries in Japanese and English throughout his life. Not surprisingly, the penmanship in both languages was textbook perfect. Kano composed many letters in both languages, grammatically correct, to the point, and easy to understand. When he spoke English, each word was pronounced clearly and distinctly. Incidentally, Kano was interested in Esperanto for a time, and toyed with the idea of trying to introduce a roman alphabet to write Japanese rather than Chinese characters (kanji) and Japanese native script (kana).

Kano was not much over five feet tall—but he was stocky, weighing about 160 pounds in his prime, with thick calves and

Kano in 1932, at age seventy-two, demonstrating shizen-tai (natural stance).

forearms. Students recall that Kano was very flexible, but as soon as he applied a technique his body seemed to turn into an iron rod. His movements were lightning fast.

Kano did not smoke, and disliked those who did; Kano drank some—a flask of sake, a bottle of beer, or a glass of wine. He did not like it at all if things got rowdy at a dinner party or banquet, and would leave immediately if he thought others were drinking too much. He told his school students, "It is better not to drink alcohol, but if you must do so, be mindful of your health, your wallet, and your behavior."

Kano could eat. He loved food of all kinds—Japanese, Chinese,

A publicity still of Kano overseeing a women's practice session, although he is looking at the camera, not the students. Notice that the female on the right is considerably bigger than her male partner.

and Western—and he was a voracious eater to the end of his days. Kano was famous for polishing off a couple of beefsteaks two or three times a week. And he loved fruit: the baggage Kano was carrying on his last voyage included five crates of oranges and one case of grapefruit.

When Kano developed diabetes in his later years, he had to watch his diet more closely, but food remained one of his greatest joys. Other than diabetes and kidney stones, Kano was healthy, and almost never went to a doctor, although he did suffer occasional food poisoning because he liked raw seafood so much. Kano had trouble with his legs in his later years and once in a while needed to be carried to an appointment or lecture on a stretcher. He liked to get moxabustion in his later years. Kano rejuvenated himself at hot springs, especially before and after long trips, where he got *amma* massages.

Kano was always impeccably dressed in either Japanese or

A publicity still of Kano teaching two children.

Western style. With the exception of a few photos taken in his student days, Kano is always shown in formal Japanese kimono; in a well-turned Western suit or frock coat with starched collar and tie; or in ceremonial garb, complete with medals and gold braid. Two well-known photos show him in his judo outfit, one standing alone in *shizen-tai* (natural stance) and one paired with Kyuzo Mifune. The majority of the judo photos we have of Kano in the second half of his life are publicity stills, staged to show the elegantly decked out Kano giving instruction to youngsters or to women, or demonstrating throws.

Kano was a bit of a dandy. He showed up at his teacher Iikubo's funeral riding a white horse in full mourning dress. Later in life, Kano cultivated a comb-over to hide his increasing baldness.

When Kano was traveling the world promoting the Olympic cause, it was necessary for him to meet all kinds of important people in the countries he visited. Most of them had heard of his reputation as the founder of Kodokan judo and his work as the Father of Japanese Sports. They expected to encounter a large, athletic-looking man, someone perhaps a bit fierce and assertive. People were surprised to be greeted by a small, elegantly dressed, distinguished gentleman with a scholarly air and a refined and polite manner of speaking. On occasion, however, mischievous "little Kano," would stun everyone by giving an extemporaneous, but good-natured, exhibition of the efficacy of judo on some unsuspecting military officer, bodyguard, or professional athlete. Kano was quite adept at charming everyone—another aspect of good judo.

Despite his extraordinary workload, Kano never complained of fatigue; he even disliked hearing the polite phrase *Otsukare-sama deshita* ("You must be very tired"). When that was said to him, Kano replied, "I'm not tired."

When he did relax, Kano enjoyed playing Go, but his opponents were often masters of the game. Although the masters were his friends, Kano no doubt tried his best to beat them. In order to do that, he had to focus intently on the game, which is complicated and demanding. Doesn't sound much like relaxing. Kano played the shakuhachi (Japanese flute) a bit and collected some antiques, particularly jade. He liked raising bonsai, nurturing trees, and watching them grow.

There were a few things that judo master Kano could not master. Although Kano grew up next to the ocean, enjoyed going to the seashore, and promoted water sports for his college students, he was never a good swimmer himself. He carried a camera with him on his overseas trips but only got one good shot out of a hundred. He was always forgetting or misplacing his keys, consequently locking himself out of house or office. A couple of times, he forgot to bring his passport with him on a trip. Eternally optimistic Kano told his anxious secretary on such occasions, "Don't worry. It will turn out fine."

As mentioned, Kano was unstintingly generous—supporting many of his students out of his own pocket, on occasion even handing his pay envelope unopened to someone in dire need—and determined to keep the Kodokan afloat. To that purpose, he used so much of his own money that he frequently found himself in financial distress because of heavy loans. Several times, in fact, Kano was in danger of having some of his property repossessed—the belongings not already in the pawnshop, that is. Near the end of Kano's life, his financial situation was so precarious that his wealthy friends and supporters were making arrangements for him to avoid bankruptcy.

In 1909, a Kodokan Foundation was established and received government approval. At first, the donors to the foundation consisted of Kano, some of his relatives, and a few wealthy members of the Kodokan. As the Kodokan increased in size and influence, the foundation began to receive financial support from various quarters—except government subsidies, because Kano did not want the Kodokan to be dependent on the government in any way, thus jeopardizing its independent status—but in Kano's lifetime it was never quite enough to keep the Kodokan debt-free. The financial situation was so bad that on the fiftieth anniversary of the Kodokan, in order to avoid bankruptcy, Kano floated a scheme to have all the black belt holders (at the time nearly forty thousand) pay the registration fee for their next rank, and everyone would be upgraded a rank. Since there was so much opposition to the plan, it was abandoned. Despite all this financial woe, the training fee at the Kodokan remained quite reasonable, due to Kano's wish to make judo accessible to anyone.

Kano's Views on Religion and Education

Kano disliked all organized religions. He thought them narrow-minded and limited in scale (not to mention too superstitious). Nonetheless, the single remaining textbook from his early student days is a copy of *Becoming a Living Buddha* by the Tendai monk Nizo. One of the sentences that the young Kano had underlined in red was, "People are always looking for riches here and there without realizing the real treasure is within."

Once, at the Tokyo Teacher Training College, a faculty member named Yamamoto arranged for a lecture series, without Principal Kano's permission, on Christianity by the Japanese minister Tokutomi. Yamamoto was called to Kano's office. "Did you ask my permission do this?" Kano inquired. Yamamoto replied, "I request permission now." Kano: "Too late. And Tokutomi cannot lecture on Christianity because that subject is too limiting. He needs to learn how to sing a different tune, about Japan's place in the modern world, not about the 'truth' of Christianity." Philosophy on the curriculum was fine with Kano, but religious propaganda—Shinto, Buddhist, and Christian—was not.

One of the pillars of Kano's educational philosophy is that education must be completely separate from religion. Instruction in ethics was necessary, but not classes in religious doctrine. The bedrock of ethics for Kano was Confucian philosophy. If there was anyone to be venerated, it was Confucius—an actual human being, who was an artist and aesthetician as well as a social thinker and educator. Kano was instrumental in reestablishing the "Confucius Festival" at Yushima Seido in 1907. Now, thanks to Kano's efforts, every April 4 there is a ceremony to commemorate Confucius, the patron of learning and rational thinking, at Yushima Hall.

In Edo Japan, primary education was conducted at schools attached to Buddhist temples and higher learning was conducted at Confucian academies. After the Meiji Restoration, it was Catholic or Protestant missionaries who established the first modern schools in Japan. Such schools had an agenda—to teach their students the missionaries' version of Christianity. In reaction to the establishment of Christian schools, Buddhist sects founded their own schools, but again the teaching was based on religious principles, not modern educational theory. Kano, head of the largest teacher training college in Japan, wanted his students to keep their religious beliefs to themselves, and at all times use a rational approach to the subjects that they were teaching. For ethics and moral education, Kano considered Confucian principles ideal.

Tetsuji Morohashi (1883–1982), a graduate of the Tokyo Teacher Training College and then a professor at the college, was the scholar who compiled the *Great Chinese-Japanese Character Dictionary* (fifteen volumes), perhaps an even more significant achievement than the compilation of the *Oxford English Dictionary*. When Morohashi was a young instructor at the college, he wanted to study in China, but the college had no funds to support study abroad. Principal Kano, who recognized Morohashi's great promise as a scholar of Chinese literature, said, "Let's see what I can do." Kano had done some favors for one of the members of the wealthy Mitsui family. When the family said they wanted to donate some money for one of Kano's projects, Kano said, "I have just the right person." Kano arranged for five hundred yen to be donated to Morohashi's scholarship fund, and then added three hundred yen himself. Morohashi was thus able to study in China for two years. Morohashi, who lived nearly one hundred years, went on to become the greatest scholar and compiler of dictionaries of Chinese literature in Japan (and perhaps in China too).

Once, Morohashi said to Kano, "Why is the school library so small? There is no reading room, so the students have to sit in chairs in the hall. On the other hand, the school has a big dojo. What's going on here?" Smiling, Kano replied, "There are many places students can read a book, but there is only one place they can practice judo." Kano's motto was, "Education is meant to make a student a better person, not a bookworm." However, Kano did find a way to get more money for the library in the next budget.

Surprisingly for a principal of a teacher training college, Kano was not a fan of book learning. He himself believed that he read too much when he was a student. He felt he should have confined his reading to his major field and not wasted time on extraneous material. (The superefficient Kano never considered that one might read a book for pleasure or general interest.) At his college, Kano considered physical education and book learning equally important. However, discouraging potential teachers—except those few like Morohashi—from reading too much seems a bit extreme.

As an educationalist, Kano adhered to the slow-but-sure approach. He made these observations:

A prodigy at five, a genius at ten, average at fifteen.
A prodigy at five, a nutcase at fifteen.
Genius is close to illness.

For Kano, true intelligence was due to diligent study and moral development, not innate ability.

With the exception of the incident with his son Riho, Kano's life seemed to be largely scandal-free, even from the three demons of ruin: money, sex, and wine. Kano selflessly used nearly all of his own money to keep the Kano Academy and the Kodokan afloat. Kano was devoted to his wife, and apparently refrained from consorting with either women or men (plus, when would he have had the time?). As noted above, Kano was a moderate and careful drinker.

Kano did like to be in charge and always believed he was right—an attitude that caused ceaseless friction with bureaucrats and his political opponents throughout his career.

Kano and Katsu Kaishu

Among Kano's Japanese mentors, Katsu Kaishu (1823–99) had the strongest influence on Kano's career. Kaishu was one of the most highly respected leaders in Meiji Japan, by Japanese and foreigners alike.

As a young samurai, Kaishu trained in swordsmanship under Shimada Toranosuke (1814–52), of the Jikishin kage ryu. Shimada was a master swordsman who also had knowledge of Kito ryu jujutsu. Additionally, Shimada had done Zazen under the direction of Sengai Gibon (1750–1837), the internationally renowned Zen master and artist. (Sengai was the one who brushed the most famous Zen painting in history, *Circle, Triangle, and Square*.) Shi-

Katsu Kaishu, the person who had the greatest and most positive influence on Kano's career.

mada told Kaishu, "If you want to master the secrets of swordsmanship, you must study Zen meditation." Shimada's primary instruction to his disciples was, "The Sword is the Mind. If the Mind is not true, the Sword will not be true. If you want to study the Sword, you must first learn about the Mind."

For four years, Kaishu divided his time between the kenjutsu dojo and the meditation hall. Every night, Kaishu sequestered himself in a mountain shrine, alternating periods of swinging his sword with periods of meditation right up to daybreak. Kaishu often commented that these years of severe training in swordsmanship and Zen enabled him to unflinchingly face the many hardships and life-threatening events of his later career.

Kaishu was Japan's first internationalist. In 1860, Kaishu commanded the *Kirin-maru* carrying the initial Japanese delegation to the United States. In the United States, Kaishu was most impressed at how of classes of people mingled together freely and how well women were treated. Thereafter, Kaishu had a long and distinguished public career, mostly in regard to the founding of the Japanese navy. Kaishu was the first minister of the navy, from 1873 to 1878.

It was Kaishu's involvement with maritime affairs that led to several visits to the Kano villa in Mikage during the 1860s. Kaishu and Jirosaku Kano (Jigoro Kano's father) discussed the development of Japan's shipping industry and the establishment of a navy. Kaishu became a friend of the Kano family, giving the eldest daughter the name "Katsuko," as well as taking the young Jigoro under his wing.

Kaishu served as the main adviser to Kano over the following decades. Kaishu provided Kano with several important examples:

Kaishu's daily study program consisted of Western learning in the morning, Chinese classics in the afternoon, and Japanese literature at night—in other words, an education combining the best of East and West. That became Kano's ideal.

Nonviolence was another pillar of Kaishu's life and teaching. In the turmoil surrounding the fall of the shogunate and the establishment of the Meiji Restoration, there was constant conflict and danger. Kaishu proudly stated, "I have been the target of at least twenty assassination attempts. I have scars all over my body. Yet I never once drew my sword in anger or revenge. The best swordsman is the one who does not need to resort to cutting and killing with a blade. Killing should be avoided at all costs." In modern Japanese history, Kaishu is remembered as the courageous mediator who negotiated the peaceful surrender of the shogunate's forces in 1867, saving Edo (Tokyo) from the death and destruction of an invasion. Later, as a government counselor, Kaishu opposed the Sino-Japanese War of 1894–95. He said, "Japan appeared to win in the short term, but continually engaging in war will eventually lead to defeat." Kaishu's nonviolent approach was Kano's guiding principle behind the establishment of Kodokan judo and his own political philosophy.

After Kano graduated from Tokyo University and secured a teaching position at the Peers School, he visited Kaishu for advice. Kano told Kaishu, "Now that I have become a teacher, I will devote all my time to study." Kaishu said, "That will not do. If you only study like that, you will turn into a bookworm, an ivory tower scholar. Study must relate to society at large; education must have practical results." That advice became Kano's standpoint as an educator.

Some other teachings of Kaishu that Kano absorbed:

Don't give yourself a way out. If you plan a way out, you will use it, sooner or later, to escape. Be resolute yet flexible, and you will never be defeated.

The more opponents, the better.

When things are too easy, nothing great can be accomplished.

Defeat comes from within, not without.

If you want to resolve a problem, tackle it head-on. Scheming will never do.

Kaishu's final words on his deathbed were: "That's it!"

Kaishu's motto: "Detached from self, in harmony with others, settled during calm, resolute during action, composed in thought, and firm during setbacks."

Kaishu supported the activities of the Kodokan over the years, appearing at all important ceremonies. Kaishu brushed the huge framed calligraphy that hung on the wall overlooking the dojo for decades. Kano donated the stone water basin (for washing the hands and rinsing the mouth) that stands before his honored teacher Kaishu's tomb.

Kano, Fenollosa, Okakura, Yanagi, and Bigelow

In the first decades of the twentieth century these five men had an incalculable effect on the social and artistic history of Japan and the West. The five were teachers, students, friends, and supporters of one another.

Ernest Fenollosa

Ernest Fenollosa, Kano's favorite professor, fell completely under the spell of his adopted country soon after his arrival in Japan in

1878. Fenollosa is recognized as a cultural hero for what he did to preserve and advance Japanese art in particular and Far East Asian art in general. Together with Kano's classmate Tenshin Okakura, Fenollosa spent years cataloging (and in many cases purchasing) the nation's art treasures.

Fenollosa himself studied Japanese painting, first with Hirotaka Sumiyoshi and Eitoku Kano and then with Kano Hogai. Hogai (1828–88), head of the three-hundred-year-old Kano school of painting, no longer had any patrons. He had put away his brushes and supported himself by selling brooms and baskets and casting iron. Fenollosa purchased some of Hogai's works and hired him as a tutor to encourage the master to begin painting again. At the time, most modernized upper-class Japanese regarded art by the Kano school as well as that of Tosa, Koetsu, and other schools as old-fashioned and uninteresting. Buddhist art was dismissed as even less worthy of serious consideration in this modern world. Fenollosa and Okakura were responsible for saving and promoting the appreciation of Japanese art at home and abroad in the context of combining the best of Eastern and Western sensitivities.

Fenollosa and Okakura and helped found the Tokyo School of Fine Arts and the Tokyo Imperial Museum. Fenollosa's own collection became the core of the Oriental Art Collection at the Museum of Fine Arts (MFA) in Boston. Fenollosa authored two classics: *The Masters of Ukiyo-e* (1896) and *Epochs of Chinese and Japanese Art* (1912). He was ordained a Tendai Buddhist priest and was granted an artist name from the Kano school of painting. In many ways, Fenollosa was more Japanese than the Japanese. His ashes are interred at Homyo-in, a subtemple of the grand Tendai temple complex of Mii-dera, at the foot of Mount Hiei.

(Kano later repaid some of his debt to his former professor by hiring Fenollosa to teach English at the Tokyo Teacher Training College from 1897 to 1900. In 1896, Fenollosa had lost his job as curator at the MFA because of a sex scandal—he divorced his wife to marry his assistant and mistress, the writer Mary McNeill Scott [1865–1954]. Fenollosa needed to get out of Boston fast.)

Tenshin Okakura

Tenshin (Kakuzo) Okakura (1862–1913), Fenollosa's collaborator and Kano's classmate and good friend, became the period's foremost art critic of Asian culture. Okakura was born in Yokohama to a family of well-off silk merchants. He started to learn English when he was six years old at the English school founded by Dr. James Curtis Hepburn (1815–1911), the missionary-linguist who established the now standard Hepburn system of romanization for Japanese. At age nine, when his father remarried, Okakura was boarded at a Buddhist temple and began the study of Chinese classics under the tutelage of the head priest. In 1875, at age twelve, Okakura was in the first class of what was to become Tokyo University. Okakura was one year ahead of Kano. At fourteen, Okakura entered the academy of Seiko Okuhara (1837–1913), the eccentric painter. (The openly gay Okuhara was equally famed as both a martial artist and a painter.)

In 1878, Okakura began practice of the koto. In 1879, when Okakura was sixteen, he married a thirteen-year-old girl named Moto. (The couple had two children by the time Okakura was twenty-two.) Okakura's first volume of Chinese-style poetry was published the same year.

After his graduation from Tokyo University in 1880, Okakura traveled with Fenollosa all over Japan and then accompanied Fenollosa to Europe and the United States to study Western art. After various posts in the Ministry of Education, Okakura became principal of the Tokyo School of Fine Arts in 1888. Following a series of scandalous events (described below), he was forced to resign as principal in 1890.

Okakura then formed his own Japan Art Institute. Okakura spent the next ten years traveling all over the world, directing the Japan Art Institute and, from 1904, working periodically as "adviser" and then, from 1910, as formal curator of Asian art at the Museum of Fine Arts in Boston. During his tenure at the MFA, Okakura cataloged in detail over 3,642 paintings. (Okakura harshly criticized

Fenollosa for acquiring [on his own] so many fakes [476] and copies [277].) When he was not traveling, Okakura stayed at his retreat at oceanside Izura in Ibaraki Prefecture. There he nourished a new generation of Japanese artists such as Taikan Yokoyama (1868–1958), Kanzan Shimomura (1873–1930), Shunso Hishida (1874–1911), and Buzan Kimura (1876–1942). Shunso Hishida—at Okakura's or Kano's request?—later composed the well-known and historically invaluable *Training at the Fujimi-cho Dojo* painting, which depicts Kano overseeing his students performing a variety of techniques.

Okakura championed the cause of Asian culture, especially art, and its importance as a counterbalance to the increasing Westernization of the globe. Okakura shared the same views as Nobel Prize winner Rabindranath Tagore, whom he met in India in 1902. (Tagore was a big fan of judo, promoting its practice at his academy. Tagore corresponded with Kano, and later met him in Tokyo.)

Okakura became an internationally renowned philosopher, art critic, and aesthete. His books *The Ideals of the East* (1903) and *The Book of Tea* (1906) are classics still in print in many languages.

Fluent in English on many levels—English was really his first language because he studied English formally before he had regular lessons in Japanese—Okakura is famous for this tale:

Okakura was in New York walking along with a few of his disciples, all dressed Japanese style. A young American on the street stopped them and asked, "Hey, what kind of nese are you people? Chinese, Japanese, or Javanese?" Okakura replied, "We are Japanese gentlemen. But what kind of key are you? Yankee, donkey, or monkey?"

The flamboyant Okakura always dressed in formal Japanese style, usually wearing a flowing cloak and Taoist hat. At his Japan Art Institute, Okakura showed up each day riding on a white horse, in a white robe, and wearing sealskin boots. When Okakura was at his oceanside retreat in Izura, he became enamored of fishing, in the manner of a Chinese scholar retired from the world and enjoying simple pursuits. The famous carving of Okakura by Denchu Hiragushi shows the elegant philosopher and aesthete in his cloak and Taoist hat but wearing straw scandals and holding a bamboo fishing pole in one hand and a basket for his catch in the other.

The constant international travel destroyed Okakura's health, and he died of heart disease and kidney failure in 1913, at the young age of fifty-one.

Okakura evidently knew some judo, since it is reported that Bigelow (see below) and Okakura demonstrated it at a few events in Boston. Okakura's obituary, written by Bigelow and John Ellerton and published in the December 1913 issue of the MFA's *Bulletin*, describes Okakura as "a past master of poetry writing and arranging flowers, music, the formal tea ceremony, fencing, and jujutsu."

Regarding Okakura's activities in Boston, mention must be made of Isabella Stewart Gardner (1840–1924). Mrs. Gardner—patron of all the arts and the most influential woman in Boston—built the fantastic Isabella Stewart Gardner Museum, a short distance from Fenway Park, to house her treasures. The building and the collection displayed within are hard to describe—eclectic, wildly eccentric, and overwhelming in scope and splendor.

Although Mrs. Gardner was in her sixties and Okakura in his late thirties, she was enthralled by the Japanese philosopher, poet, and art critic. Mrs. Gardner fell completely under Okakura's spell. Their deep and romantic relationship was the talk of Boston. Mrs. Gardner was devastated by Okakura's early death in 1913.

What most concerns us here, however, is Mrs. Gardner's relationship to judo. In the music room of her mansion, she had at least one demonstration of judo—perhaps one by Okakura and Bigelow—and there is some evidence that the athletic Mrs. Gardner practiced judo herself, becoming quite good at it. It is not unlikely that Okakura taught her some judo.

Like Fenollosa (and unlike Kano), Okakura's brilliant career was marred by a sex scandal, one of the most tragic of modern times. In 1887, Okakura's patron Ryuichi Kuki (1850–1931), then serving as Japanese ambassador to the United States, asked Okakura to accompany his ailing wife, Hatsu (1860–1931), back to Japan. Hatsu, a lovely former geisha, fell deeply in love with Okakura. (As noted, she was hardly the first or last; Okakura proved irresistible to many women.) Even when Kuki found out about the affair, he was reluctant to let his wife go and refused to divorce her. Hatsu had borne a son, Shunzo (later to become a well-known philosopher), in 1888. Regardless of his actual paternity—she may have already been pregnant before the affair started—Shunzo always considered Okakura his real father. When Hatsu's affair with Okakura became public, Okakura had to resign as principal of the Tokyo School of Fine Arts. Hatsu and Ryuichi finally divorced in 1900. Although Okakura continued to visit Hatsu regularly for many years, they never married.

Sadly, Hatsu never recovered from her love affair with Okakura. In 1906, Ryuichi and other family members were able to get her committed to a mental hospital. She was in and out of the hospital until her death in 1931.

Soetsu Yanagi

Okakura's spiritual successor was Soetsu Yanagi (1889–1961). Yanagi too was a philosopher of international reputation, art critic, and founder of the Mingei movement. In the realm of folk art and crafts, Yanagi was as influential as Okakura. Yanagi authored the other classic book on Japanese aesthetics *The Unknown Craftsman*. Yanagi's writings had a profound impact on the appreciation of both Japanese and world folk art and crafts.

Yanagi was Kano's nephew. His mother was Kano's sister Katsuko Yanagi. After Soetsu's father died when Soetsu was two years old, Kano helped support the family through very difficult times. As mentioned, Kano lived with the Yanagi family in 1891. Later, in 1911, Kano built a family retreat in Abiko, Chiba Prefecture, and let Yanagi live there. Yanagi helped establish Abiko as the center of the Shirakaba movement. The Shirakaba group consisted of Yanagi and other progressive young writers, philosophers, and aestheticians. The group published the highly influential journal *Shirakaba*, containing many important articles by

Yanagi. Yanagi also published his private journal "Letters from Abiko" between 1913 and 1914. In a sense, no Jigoro Kano, no Soetsu Yanagi.

William Sturgis Bigelow

William Sturgis Bigelow (1860–1931) was a millionaire physician who had a wide influence on the arts and politics of the day. He was the chief patron of Fenollosa and Okakura, and introduced Theodore Roosevelt to judo. Bigelow came to Japan a little later than Fenollosa, in 1882, but fell just as much in love with the country and its culture. Bigelow was ordained a Tendai Buddhist priest together with Fenollosa. In 1908, he published a book entitled *Buddhism and Immortality* and later articles on "The Method of Practicing Concentration and Contemplation, by Chisha Daishi, translated by Okakura" and "The Relation of Samadhi to the Normal Waking Consciousness." Bigelow was a lifelong friend and supporter of both Fenollosa and Okakura and was the main financial contributor to Okakura's Japan Art Institute. He got Fenollosa and Okakura curator jobs at the MFA in Boston, to which Bigelow had donated his huge forty-thousand-object collection of Japanese art.

On the US political front, Bigelow and the prominent senator Henry Cabot Lodge (1850–1924) considered Theodore Roosevelt their protégé, and the pair had tremendous influence on the president. Bigelow had learned some judo in Japan during his seven-year stay there, and in 1902 demonstrated the art to the president—Bigelow pinned the secretary of war, Elihu Root, in Roosevelt's office. Bigelow then arranged for Roosevelt to be taught by the American jujutsu man J. J. O'Brien and later by the Kodokan's Yoshitsugu Yamashita.

Bigelow was gay. He never married, and only male friends were invited to his summer retreat on Tuckernuck Island, near Nantucket. The group of men spent most of their stay frolicking nude or seminude.

As we can see, the lives of Kano, Fenollosa, Okakura, Yanagi, and Bigelow are intricately bound; it is impossible to talk about one without mentioning the others. In many ways, together and individually, each man left a legacy that continues to benefit both Japan and the world at large.

Kano's Influence on Other Artists

Kano had an influence on the literary giants Soseki Natsume (1867–1916) and Ogai Mori (1862–1922). Kano counseled Soseki on his teaching career and even hired him (when no one else would) as a part-time instructor at Tokyo Teacher Training College. Kano told him, "You think too much and lack enthusiasm for teaching, but I am confident you can become an educator." Soseki mentioned Kano and judo in his writings. Ogai is thought to have based the character Ishihara in his novel *Geese* on Kano. Mori once invited Kano to lecture on the serious "yellow peril problem," and discussed this issue and many others with Kano. Inazo Nitobe (1862–1933), author of *Bushido*, was the principal of Tokyo Teacher Training College in the decade after Kano. Nitobe mentions jujutsu (he was probably referring to judo), but not Kano specifically. Kano and Nitobe considered judo the practical expression of the samurai spirit in the modern world.

Kano was a longtime friend and supporter of Wakamatsu Wakatayu I (1874–1948), the man responsible for reviving Sekkyo Bushi, puppet theater with a Buddhist theme. Kano often engaged Wakamatsu for both private and public events. Wakamatsu was a master storyteller, humorous and insightful. He used both traditional tales and his own compositions, and his puppet plays always had a moral (Kano liked that element). Wakamatsu's koto playing was so rich in tone, it was said that the strings of his instrument were made of gold. During the war, he abandoned performing and worked as a farmer. Wakamatsu was found by some former fans, and started to perform again. When he learned of the severe food shortages affecting the country, Wakamatsu declared, "If children do not have enough to eat, how can I?" He slowly starved to death, passing away in 1948.

In both his public career and his private life, Kano was the consummate "Meiji man." The outstanding men and women of this period in Japan believed that with hard work, anything could be accomplished. They were keenly aware of the need for Japan to be modernized, but equally convinced that the traditional values of Japanese culture had to be renewed and maintained. They were internationalists who wanted the best for the entire world. Such was the purpose of Kano's life.

3

The Challenge of Creating
Kodokan Judo

◉

IN HIS EARLY DAYS, Kano trained in jujutsu as if his life depended
upon it, but he never practiced jujutsu to the exclusion of everything else. His jujutsu training, and later his Kodokan teaching,
was always conducted in conjunction with full-time work as a college student and then as an educator. Judo was to be practiced as
one of the things a cultured person did, not the only thing. Later,
when the Kodokan had so many members that full-time instructors were necessary, Kano was not entirely happy about that development. In the back of Kano's mind was the worry: "It is not
good to do nothing but judo training always on the mat. People
get warped being in the dojo all the time. The ideal instructor
needs some kind of outside occupation as well."

Even after Kano opened the Kodokan in 1882, he continued
to train with his best students to further refine and develop the
technical aspect of Kodokan judo. When Kano himself did engage in randori with a student, it was said to be like "fighting
an empty jacket." Kano's own judo was very quick, precise, and
decisive. His hip throws accompanied by leg sweeps were especially powerful. Hip throws remain the staple of Kodokan judo
to this day. Kano himself stopped doing randori in his midthir-
ties—he had already engaged in enough matches to last a lifetime. Once in a while, Kano did show off. When the students
asked him about old-time techniques, he told five of them to pin
him with full force on the ground. With a sharp *kiai*, he threw

all of them off, stood up, and said, "That's the kind of thing we practiced."

Developing Kata

The process of formulating Kodokan judo was ongoing. Kano was the inspirational presence in the Kodokan, but the technical aspect of judo was developed by committee, based on the research of Kano himself and that of his senior instructors. The primary concern for Kano regarding both kata and randori techniques was, "If it is not safe, it is not judo. If the movements do not utilize all the body's muscles in a balanced manner, it is not judo."

Although the Judo Medical Research Group was not formally established until 1932, the following twelve areas of investigation show how deeply Kano was concerned with the safety and well-being of Kodokan judo trainees:

1. The proper application and effect of warming-up and cooling-down exercises
2. The evaluation of judo instruction of youth during their period of physical development
3. Medical evaluation of the physical and psychological effects of the cold-weather and hot-weather intense training periods
4. Judo training and physiology
5. Medical research on the practical implications of the *seiryoku-zenyo-kokumin-taiku* exercises
6. Medical evaluation of the stress on the bones and joints from particular techniques
7. The medical implications of chokes resulting in unconsciousness and subsequent recovery
8. The effects of atemi, physically and psychologically
9. Evaluation of the type and frequency of judo injuries
10. Statistical analysis of the life expectancy of judo practitioners
11. Dojo hygiene
12. Medical ramifications for female judo practitioners

The Demands of Competition

Kano was constantly tweaking the technical curriculum in response to the demands of competition. The most dangerous techniques—punching, kicking, most joint locks, arm bars, and chokes—were gradually weeded out. In 1899, locks applied to fingers, wrists, toes, ankles, and the neck were prohibited. In 1902, it was bear hugs and leg scissor squeezes to the body that were banned, and by 1909, all leg and knee locks were eliminated.

At first, Kano emphasized randori, but then realized that trainees needed kata, set forms, a "grammar" that would help them build a balanced approach to training that Kano wanted for his Kodokan judo trainees. Also, kata provided Kodokan members with a safe method for practicing the techniques prohibited or not practical in randori. Kano and his senior disciples introduced these main kata:

1. *Randori-no-kata*:
   a. *Nage-no-kata* (throws)
   b. *Katame-no-kata* (pins, joint locks, chokes)
   These kata are reference points for randori—that is, techniques that are permitted in a match.
2. *Kime-no-kata* (combative forms for self-defense, from both armed and unarmed attacks).
3. *Ju-no-kata* (soft-style forms based on the principle of nonresistance).
4. *Go-no-kata* (hard-style forms based on attack).
5. *Itsutsu-no-kata* (the five forms). These were introduced by Kano in 1887. He worked on the five forms throughout his life—in his last years, he joked, "I've finally gotten three of them learned." The movements are simple, very subtle, based on universal principles: the flexible defeats the rigid; the best way of winning is not to fight; the tight inner circle of a whirlpool controls the huge outer circle until they become one movement; the ebb and flow of the tide purifies the world; and the disastrous collision of two forces in motion can be

avoided if one force skillfully yields in order to save both. This kata should be performed as fine art as well as martial art.

6. *Koshiki-no-kata* (old-style kata). These are old-style forms derived from the Kito ryu. Many of the movements are similar to those employed in aikido, which is not surprising since Morihei Ueshiba also trained in the Kito ryu. When Kano did formally demonstrate, it was typically the koshiki-no-kata. He continued demonstrating this kata to the end of his life.

7. *Seiryoku-zenyo-kokumin-taiku* (judo gymnastics that are executed in both an individual form and a *sotai* form in which one imagines he or she is training with a partner).

8. *Goshinho kata* (self-defense methods for men and for women).

Kano continued to introduce and revise new kata. As usual, he was never completely satisfied; he always intended to add more forms to the itsutsu no kata, so that is why that form is called the "unfinished kata." Among other reasons, Kano felt kata to be important for judo since they could be practiced up to old age, whereas randori had less and less appeal as one grew older. A few instructors, such as Mifune, created their own kata. Other instructors, though, held the opinion that "kata practice is for sissies."

There never was a uniform system of technical judo at the Kodokan, for either the techniques or the kata. Each of Kano's senior instructors had their individual style and their own interpretation of the techniques that they passed on to their respective students. Early on, there were definite factions in the Kodokan, the disciples of So-and-So Sensei pitted against the disciples of So-and-So Sensei. The rivalries were intense and often personal. However, no matter how skilled these instructors were, they were not Kano—the man, not the martial artist.

Formal Competition

From his forties on, Kano devoted himself to codifying the kata, making adjustments to the randori guidelines, giving demonstrations and lectures. While Kano would never say it expressly, his later lectures and essays give the distinct impression that he had begun to wonder, "Have I created a monster?" The primary problem was the introduction of formal competition. The first formal competitions in the Kodokan were the Monthly Tournament and the biannual Red and White Teams Tournament, first held in 1884. Then tournaments followed between schools, between districts, and eventually between nations (coming into being after Kano's death). This is how Kano wanted a contest to be: "A contest is a learning process for oneself and one's opponent. Do not be elated by a win, or disappointed by a loss. Do not relax if your opponent is weak; do not be afraid if he is strong. The single goal is to find the right path for each other." He said, "I instituted formal competition not to show a student how to win at any cost but how to lose with grace and humility."

Unfortunately, as soon as formal competition was introduced, people wanted to compete, and rivalries between high school, college, and eastern Japan and western Japan Kodokan judo teams became intense. Quickly, winning became the sole focus of the contest; it was no longer a matter of mutual give-and-take, a learning experience, as Kano intended it to be. It was a battle. It was not a question of winning fair and square; it was an issue of winning by any means possible. When that becomes the goal, competitors train in their favorite techniques to the exclusion of others, thus creating a one-dimensional judo man. A competitor tries to apply his favorite technique, appropriate or not. Competitors are constantly getting hurt. (Sadly, I heard a university coach tell the members of his judo team, "If you are *not* getting injured, it is not judo. If you are not getting hurt, it means you are not practicing hard enough.")

Kano wanted Kodokan trainees to compete sincerely without regard to results. He told his academic students the same thing: "You are not here studying to someday become prime minister or a wealthy businessman. You are here to find your own path in life, to learn what is best for you, not to be concerned if your grades are better than others'!" Kano was said not to have released his students' report cards until they graduated to prevent them from competing against one another for higher marks.

For Kano, randori was an educational vehicle. Competitors bow to each other at the beginning and end of the match. This bow is an expression of respect and gratitude. The opponents are thanking each other for the opportunity to improve their technique, win or lose. Kano advised competitors to accommodate each other. Give each other an opportunity to try their best techniques to see if they worked or not in a particular situation. The best way to win is not to fear losing. A strictly defensive posture maintained throughout a match is a defeat, regardless of any points scored. A win must be in a manner that is natural, refined, and dignified.

A competitor will never be considered a winner if he has resorted to brute strength, dirty tricks, or employs a big height or weight advantage to stifle his opponent. The best victory in randori is achieved with just the right amount of force—neither too much nor too little, neither too fast nor too slow.

Here is a summary of Kano's statements on the "Purpose of Kodokan Judo" and the "Deterioration of Randori" (entries twenty-three and twenty-four in his memoirs):

The purpose of Kodokan judo is physical education, how to behave in contests, how to cultivate wisdom and virtue, and the application of judo principles to daily life. Judo training builds the body, contests build the spirit. The judo spirit consists of perseverance, self-restraint, good manners, and respect for others. The purpose of Kodokan judo is to bring out the best in a person. It is for enabling one to lead a satisfying and meaningful life. In contests, flexibility, agility, and polished movements are preferable to brute strength and excessive use of overdeveloped musculature. Contests are to be conducted according to the highest standards of moral behavior; a contest should be a learning experience that improves your character, not an occasion for building your ego. This is what I have taught from the beginning of the Kodokan, but fewer and fewer students seem to be listening. Randori now is not what I intended it to be.

I introduced competition in Kodokan judo as an educational tool to give trainees an opportunity to hone their physical and mental abilities in a public forum. Unfortunately, contests have become increasingly competitive, winning now being the most important factor among the majority of trainees. I have not been able to transmit my ideals to many students, and there are unfortunately few instructors who can impart proper Kodokan values. Randori has largely become "strength versus strength" wrestling matches. Kodokan judo has gotten out of hand.

Kano also mentions the perennial problem of contest rules. The establishment of contest rules was a constant headache for Kano. In 1890, the first Kodokan rules were issued: Wins were by two *ippons*, either by a clean throw, a pin, or submission by a choke or joint lock. Contests had a fifteen-minute time limit. There had to be a greater percentage of standing techniques versus groundwork grappling. However, the rules were continually revised; techniques that were too dangerous were eliminated, contests were shortened, guidelines were issued for awarding points, penalties were established for infractions, and provisions were made for injuries. Then, of course, there was the matter of how these rules were applied by the referee—strictly or loosely—and if his judgment was sound; was it a clean throw or not? Worse were contests that had to be decided by *hantei*, "judges' decision." In team tournaments, there can be contests that end in a draw, but in an individual tournament, there *must* be a winner and loser. Even with the introduction of a "sudden-death" period if the regular match ends without conclusive results, at the end there are times when the competitors are simply an even match. As in any sport where a contest is decided by a judgment call, such decisions are nearly always questioned; there will always be onlookers who consider the call "unfair."

Regarding formal competition taking place within the Japanese judo community, there was the "1918 Tokyo High School versus Sendai High School Tournament affair," which Kano felt compelled to comment on. The coach at the Sendai High School, third dan Tsunetane Ota (1892–1955), a master of groundwork, made his judo club members train exclusively on groundwork techniques five or six hours a day. Ota was clever. He knew from personal experience how weak Tokyo Kodokan judo fighters were on the ground. When he was in Tokyo, Ota won almost all of his matches on the ground—his specialty being the "hell choke."

In the contests, as soon as the match went to the ground, the Sendai crew were able to handily defeat the Tokyo High School members, even those of higher ranks, with their superior groundwork. Kano, who was in attendance, was shocked at the results and the fact that several of the Tokyo team members had their shoulders dislocated by pins. Immediately, there was controversy: "What good is a ranking system if white belts (from the sticks) can beat first dan and second dan black belts (from Tokyo)?"

Kano defended the ranking system, maintaining that ranks are not presented only on technical ability or on the number of victories attained in a tournament. Also, it is contrary to the spirit of judo to train only to emerge victorious in contests. "Winning by any means" is not what judo contests are about. Judo training and contests need to be concentrated on standing techniques and throws, not groundwork. That is the message Kano always tried to convey, with varied success. Among other things, Kano felt that groundwork is vulnerable if kicks or punches to the head were allowed in the matches. And of course groundwork is only applicable in a one-on-one situation contested on a mat. It is useless if there is more than one opponent or if the match is being fought on rocky ground or other rough surfaces. Kano was never able to convince several of his instructors to place less emphasis on groundwork. "Groundwork judo" (Kosen judo) continues to be the primary focus of certain judo schools, especially in the Kansai area. Overseas, groundwork has always been the mainstay of judo men in open contests against wrestlers and other types of fighters.

We can tell from the number of lectures and articles that Kano continually addressed to his Kodokan followers that he was trying to put Kodokan contests back in the proper perspective. Contests were only one aspect of Kodokan judo; winning was not the primary purpose of a contest, it was educational; placing first in a tournament should never be the single-minded focus of training. Ideally, the best contest is a draw; that means the competitors were evenly matched. The more techniques in one's arsenal, the better, but self-perfection is the best weapon.

Dissention in the Kodokan

There were Kodokan instructors who disagreed publicly with Kano's view of competition. They argued, "Judo is for competition. Right from the start, a student should train to win in a contest. If you learn to win a contest, you can learn to win at anything. That perfection-of-character stuff can come later. A judo man needs practice, not theory." After outbursts such as this, Kano realized that he had not trained his instructors properly.

The leader of the anti-Kano faction in the Kodokan was Heita Okabe (1891–1966). Okabe was extraordinarily skilled at judo, on a par with Kyuzo Mifune. Okabe, born in Fukuoka, was a gifted athlete in middle and high school, participating in both Western sports such as baseball and soccer, and Japanese sports such as sumo and jujutsu. In 1913, Okabe entered both Tokyo Teacher Training College and the Kodokan. Okabe had obtained first dan in a local dojo. A few weeks after he entered the Kodokan, there was the regular Kohaku Competition. When Okabe showed up wearing a black belt, Sakujiro Yokoyama, the head instructor, told him to take it off. Okabe stunned everyone by throwing five opponents in a row, thus earning a Kodokan judo second dan on the spot. Seven months later, he was third dan and then fourth dan in May 1914. Okabe went from first dan to fourth dan in a year, the fastest track ever.

Okabe was once Kano's pet student. He arranged for Okabe to study physical education at the University of Chicago in the United States. Okabe played everything—basketball, baseball, track and field, American football, and tennis. He visited boxing and wrestling clubs. Johnny Weissmuller coached him in swimming. When Okabe returned to Japan, he was convinced that judo should be conducted as a competitive sport along the same lines as all other sports.

Okabe was the central figure in the "Santel affair." Ad Santel (1888–1966), an American catch wrestler, had defeated several men claiming to be judo fighters, one an unknown college student named Fukuda and the other a self-proclaimed eighth dan master, Senryuken Noguchi, who was actually a jujutsu practitioner. However, judo fifth dan Tokugoro Ito was the real deal. In February 1916, Santel defeated Ito by TKO at a well-publicized wrestling match (punches and kicks were prohibited) held in San Francisco. The question raised was: "Doesn't Ito's defeat reflect badly on the quality of Kodokan judo's techniques?"

The Kodokan's disingenuous reply: "Ito had been away from Japan for so long, his technical ability in judo had declined; fifth dan is only a middle-level rank; it was Ito's fault he lost, not judo's." However, Kano, who had met Ito in San Francisco and traveled with him throughout California, was in fact well aware of Ito's ability in judo. It must be said that Kano was overconfident about the innate superiority of Japanese Kodokan fighters. He believed that even if a Japanese fighter was only equal or slightly inferior technically to a non-Japanese fighter, he would always win "through the Japanese virtues of diligence and hard work." (Or if a foreigner defeated the Japanese judo man, it was always because he was so much bigger, turning the defeat into a moral victory.)

Ito had engaged in hundreds of professional contests, frequently all-comers-welcome brawls, emerging victorious in virtually all of them thanks to his judo skills. He was as much a fighter as anyone in the Kodokan. Ito, in fact, redeemed himself in a rematch with Santel a few months later, choking him out in the third round. (Santel stated that he had three matches in all: a win for him, a win for Ito, and a draw.)

After defeating two other skilled judo men—third dan Taro Miyake and fourth dan Daisuke Sakai—in Seattle at the end of

1917, Santel, with the help of Okabe, decided to go to Japan and issue a direct challenge to the Kodokan.

It was not until early 1921 that Santel, accompanied by another wrestler, Henry Weber, made it to Japan. Initially, Okabe promoted the challenge matches as a "Japan-U.S.A. Friendship Competition." Santel was greeted at the Yokoyama pier by a contingent from the Kodokan that included Yamashita, the head instructor. However, Kano, who had been out of the country while all this transpired, was not pleased when he found out about the matches upon his return to Japan only two weeks before Santel had arrived. He complained that he had not been properly consulted beforehand. Kano refused to have the Kodokan sanction the matches, saying that they would create a spectacle and that such fights for money in front of a rabble-rousing audience were contrary to the Kodokan spirit. Kano threatened Okabe and anyone who organized or engaged in a match with Santel with expulsion from the Kodokan.

Of course, Kano knew quite well that judo men could not let such a challenge go unanswered. By not sanctioning the matches, the Kodokan could claim that because the judo men were not official representatives, it was their fault if they lost and thus did not reflect upon the quality of Kodokan judo.

Matches were finally arranged so each of the challengers would fight on the card against judo men. The matches were to be held, outside of Kodokan auspices, at the giant sumo ring at Yasukuni Shrine, the center of patriotic Japan.

The first day, March 5, pitted Henry Weber against second dan Shotaro Musuda and Ad Santel against third dan Reijiro Nagata. It was a spectacle, with a crowd of ten thousand, a host of dignitaries, and a brass band.

Blond-haired Weber was six feet tall, weighed two hundred pounds, and looked like a Greek god. Weber quickly got choked out in the first round but won the second by a fall. The third was a draw, but by the rules of the game, the fighter who won the first round was declared the winner. The crowd did not know the rules and thought the contest was a draw. And when they found out that Masuda was the winner, they were not pleased because Masuda had spent the third round mostly running away from Weber to protect his lead.

Next it was Santel against Reijiro Nagata. The first round was a draw, with most of the fighting on the ground. In the second round, Santel got Nagata in a crushing headlock and the match was stopped. Great confusion ensued, with the Japanese side claiming that Santel had used an illegal hold and should be disqualified. The Santel side said that their fighter had applied a standard wrestling hold. At any rate, Santel agreed that the match could continue, but Nagata was in no shape to go on. It was a TKO.

The second day had Weber against third dan Hajime Shimizu and Santel against fourth dan Hiroo Shoji. In the first match, Shimizu was the clear winner, finishing off Weber with a joint lock in both the first and second rounds. Weber lacked Santel's experience with judo fighters, and he was easy prey against a skilled judo man such as Shimizu.

Santel used his experience with judo fighters to stifle Shoji. The match was declared a draw after three rounds, but Shoji could not stand at the end and had to be helped up by Santel. The consensus was, even by Shoji himself, that Santel had the better of it. Refreshingly, Shoji did not make excuses: "Santel's wrestling moves were as good as my judo techniques, and a few were better. I need to learn more wrestling."

More matches were held in Nagoya and Osaka later that month. In Nagoya, Santel defeated Hajime Shimizu, and Weber drew with second dan Masuda. In Osaka, with the same fighters, both matches ended in draws. (Much later, in 1926, Santel had a match with fourth dan Setsuzo Ota. The match ended in a draw, but Santel said that Ota was the best Kodokan judo fighter he had ever faced. For his part, Ota remarked, "That guy is really strong. He nearly killed me.")

Kano condemned the whole affair (even though he knew it was going to take place whether he liked it or not), primarily because it turned Kodokan judo into a form of entertainment to make money and amuse audiences. In a sweeping statement, Kano maintained, "Most professional wrestlers are of low character, looked down on by society." Further, "Participation in professional matches will turn Kodokan judo men into fighters and entertainers first, not individuals seeking development of character and moral sense through training." Thus, Kano revoked the ranks of Okabe and the other six Kodokan members who organized or fought in the matches.

Okabe protested his expulsion from the Kodokan as unfair because Kodokan members such as Tokugoro Ito had been fighting professionally for years overseas without any sanctions. Okabe stated that the real reason for their expulsion was that the matches were held in Japan, and that the Kodokan fighters did not do well because they had not trained to compete against other styles of fighting. Okabe argued that Kodokan judo should become a sport, pure and simple.

From Kano's standpoint, the entire affair was an unpleasant reminder that the Kodokan was drifting further and further away from its original purpose. He was constantly reprimanding his instructors, "What you are all doing is not judo!"

(Okabe gave up judo to become the czar of modern competitive sports in Japan, especially the marathon. The intense Okabe was said never to have looked happy in his entire life.)

Judo versus Wrestling

In fact, as Kano feared, soon a few senior Kodokan men were doing more wrestling than judo. Shoji practiced wrestling with Santel when Shoji went to the United States to study. When he came back to Japan, Shoji, together with Ichiro Hatta (1906–83), became pioneers of amateur wrestling in Japan. In 1929, on a tour of the United States, Hatta's Waseda University judo team, with members ranking from fifth to third dan, squared off against the University of Washington wrestling squad with mixed results—winning two matches, drawing three—even though the U. of W.

team members were of comparatively low level. Impressed at what wrestling could do, Hatta set up a wrestling club at Waseda in 1931. Hatta practiced judo and wrestling concurrently, albeit more wrestling than judo. Hatta quickly organized a Japanese team comprised of judo members to compete in the wrestling division of the 1932 Olympics. Despite the fact that the Japanese team included skilled judo men of high rank, lead by Sumiyuki Kotani, sixth dan and at his peak, they went nowhere in the games. Although Hatta served as Kano's secretary for a brief period, he was obviously more interested in promoting judo as a competitive sport along the same lines as wrestling, and wrestling itself as an independent sport. Hatta was the coach of the Japanese wrestling contingent at the 1936 Olympics.

Hatta became a fanatical trainer of his athletes. Training to win was everything. He told his trainees to think, even dream, only about winning. To toughen them up, Hatta had them swim in the ice-cold ocean on New Year's Day and in summer sleep in the dojo without mosquito netting. His first greeting to them was not "Good morning," but "Did you have a good shit?" (an indication of healthy digestion). Before competition, he monitored every aspect of an athlete's life: the exact amount and kind of food and drink taken, how many times and what amount of urine and stool they passed, how often and how much they ejaculated during wet dreams, masturbation, and—god forbid—sex with another person. He made them go to the zoo and attempt to stare down lions. Any of his competitors who lost had to shave all the hair on their body as a mark of shame. That is not the kind of Kodokan judo instructor Kano wanted.

What did Kano regard as the ideal judo instructor? In Kodokan circles, Kano is always referred to as *Shihan*, which means "role model." Kano was looked upon as the standard for a judo instructor. It goes without saying that the instructor needs to be competent in all aspects of technical judo, but he should also have a detailed knowledge of physical education and teaching methods. The instructor should be well versed in the liberal arts, including poetry and aesthetics. He must be able to engage in dialogue—the Japanese term, taken from Zen Buddhism, is *mondo*, "question and answer"—with his students, and reply to all their inquiries until they are satisfied with the answers.

The instructor's moral behavior must be above reproach. The instructor must be experienced in applying the principles of Kodokan judo to daily life. The instructor and his or her students must set an example for society. An ideal instructor develops an ideal student: of sturdy physique, with a healthy lifestyle, morally responsible, and firm in character. Above all, judo instructors should never lose their temper and become violent and abusive. Kano himself was a gentle man, never injuring an opponent on purpose, and even avoiding harm to insects.

Although instructors are not teaching for money, professional instructors should expect to be compensated for their efforts with a salary that allows them to have sufficient food for their family, adequate housing, enough for the basic expenses of life, plus a little left over. To demand a more opulent lifestyle is an unacceptable luxury. Living up to these dictates of Kano is a tall order, but it is the ideal Kano held out for his instructors to aspire to reach. That is the reason Kano is the only one referred to in Kodokan judo as Shihan, the role model of role models.

Actually, as we shall see, Kano was quite tolerant of his instructors' and students' bad behavior. He had to suspend or expel quite a few—even senior instructors—for infractions against the Kodokan rules (and on occasion for criminal acts), but he never gave up on anyone. He allowed those who sincerely regretted and apologized for their misbehavior back into the Kodokan. One of the possible interpretations of the *ju* in *judo* is "tolerant." Kano always felt that observance of Kodokan principles could help miscreants mend their ways, sooner or later.

Kodokan Guidelines

Kano continually issued revised regulations for the Kodokan, guidelines for promotion, rules for contests, codes of behavior for Kodokan instructors, and templates for regional Kodokan organizations. The dan ranking system that Kano introduced in 1883 as an educational and promotional guideline was finalized in 1931. Beginners wore a white belt. There were ten dan ranks. First to sixth dan holders wore a black belt; sixth dan to ninth dan, a red-and-white striped belt; and tenth dan, a solid red one. There was provision for promotion to twelfth dan; tellingly, that grade belt was pure white, indicating that a master of that rank had come full circle, returning to "beginner's mind." However, no one was promoted up to twelfth dan by Kano in his lifetime. As the founder, Kano himself was outside of the ranking system, but the Kodokan posthumously promoted him to twelfth dan anyway. Kano usually wore a white belt but was photographed wearing a black one as well.

While the Kodokan ranking system worked fairly well as a reflection of technical skill and years and intensity of training, the other rules and regulations of the Kodokan were never satisfactory to either Kano or the Kodokan members for various reasons. Some instructors complained about the large number of "Do this, don't do that" regulations and rules: "We are trying to train fighters, not raise pets." Kano had instructors such as Okabe, who argued with him that judo had turned into a sport anyway, so why not build first-class competitors with weight-class divisions? Then more judo people could compete in tournaments.

At one Kodokan committee meeting regarding such guidelines, two instructors, Ikkan Miyagawa and Sakuzo Uchida, got into a violent argument. The incensed Miyagawa hurled a heavy ashtray at Uchida, striking Uchida in the forehead and drawing blood. The other instructors present prevented the two men from coming to blows. Kano was horrified. If such an incident were widely reported, it would besmirch the Kodokan's reputation (not to mention ruin the reelection chances of Miyagawa, who was running for a seat in the lower house of the Diet). It was with the greatest of difficulty that Kano persuaded Uchida not to press charges against Miyagawa and sue him. Kano realized that that the Kodokan was not developing the way he wanted.

Kano was certainly not the first person to have the organization he founded turn into something completely different from what he intended. In a sense, the success of Kodokan judo was its failure. There was a disastrous loss of what we would nowadays call "quality control." The more Kodokan students there were, the less direct contact Kano had not only with them but also with the instructors. He complained that there were not enough qualified instructors—that is, trained and supervised by Kano—to go around. Everybody was going his own way. No one was listening. At he end of his life, Kano sadly realized that he was losing the battle to other forces in the Kodokan organization.

As we have seen, the competitive side of Kodokan judo had spun out of control even during Kano's lifetime, and that aspect of judo has not gotten any better. Every serious judo competitor today can easily recount dozens of ploys and dirty tricks that have been employed against them in matches, the most innocuous being wearing a judogi two sizes too small, making it impossible to grasp, and cultivating the foulest of breath. Certain decisions made by judges on the international stage, in the World Championships and the Olympics, have caused an uproar, creating in a few cases an international incident. (Speaking of the Olympics, recently a Jigoro Kano Memorial International Sport Institute has been established in Tokyo to promote the cause of the games. Tellingly, the current chair of the board of directors is also the president of the Japan Anti-doping Agency. The biggest problem today in sports on all levels is doping—that is to say, cheating.)

Despite all this, there are and always have been countless judo practitioners, past and present, who train in the manner that Kano intended. Their Kodokan judo is for physical well-being, self-cultivation, and benefit to society. Kano set the bar very high, but his example and teachings are always there to inspire us, whether we be judo practitioners or on another Path.

4

Kano and His Students

◉

KANO'S CAREER as an educator—director of the Kodokan, principal of the Tokyo Teacher Training College, and headmaster of the Kobun Gakuen—is largely defined by the careers of his students. There is a saying: "If you want to understand a teacher, look at his or her students." It is impossible to talk about Kano without discussing his students. Many of his students—whose ranks include two prime ministers of Japan, the judo teacher of a president of the United States, and the "man who molded Mao Zedong"—played key roles in modern world history. Given the extent of Jigoro Kano's influence on so many colorful and significant characters, at home and abroad, it is essential to include a chapter that relates the fascinating stories of some of Kano's top students.

The Four Kings

In the earliest days of the Kodokan, there was a group known as the "Four Kings": Tsunejiro Tomita, Shiro Saigo, Sakujiro Yokoyama, and Yoshitsugu Yamashita. The kings were instrumental in the creation of Kodokan judo. Tomita was the "crash-test dummy," the student who trained the most with Kano, the one on whom Kano tested the techniques. The extremely talented Saigo was the one who kept Kano on his toes. Kano had to continually refine and perfect his throwing techniques to stay one step ahead of Saigo. Rough and tough Yokoyama was the traditional jujutsu man who insisted that judo must continue to be an effective martial art. Yamashita was the judo philosopher and aesthete who supported Kano in his quest to make judo a way of life as well as beautiful to behold.

Tsunejiro Tomita

In June 1882, the seventeen-year-old Tsunejiro Tomita (1865–1937), at that time Yamada, was the first to enter the Kodokan as a live-in student, at the recommendation of Kano's father. Tomita was born in Numazu in Shizuoka to a family engaged in agriculture and inn keeping. Tomita was only five years younger than Kano, and the two spent hours together training and testing various jujutsu techniques as Kano developed Kodokan judo. Some of Kano's friends wondered, "Why is he spending so much time with that country bumpkin?"

Of all of Kano's students, Tomita spent by far the most time directly training with the head of the Kodokan. Although the bookish Tomita—he later became a professor of English—was considered to be less physically gifted and technically skilled than the other kings, in 1884 he was able to prevail over giant Hansuke Nakamura, the "Demon-Slayer," of the Ryoshinto ryu, in an early challenge match, thus greatly enhancing the prestige of the fledgling Kodokan. At the grand opening of a new Tenjin Shin'yo ryu dojo, Nakamura, who was a guest, issued an impromptu challenge to Tomita, who was also a guest. It was rather unusual to have two guests from the audience go at it in a match. Tomita was up to the challenge: he managed to throw the surprised Nakamura twice and then choke him out.

Unfortunately, Tomita is best remembered for losing to other giants when he went to America. Tomita traveled to the United States in early 1905 with the intent of settling there to teach judo. Among other qualifications, Tomita spoke excellent English. However, since he was forty years old at the time, a bit past his prime, and with a permanently injured shoulder, the powerful fighters fourth dan Mitsuyo Maeda and third dan Shinshiro Satake accompanied Tomita. Tomita was supposed to do the explaining while Maeda and Satake handled the challenges. Understandably, onlookers wanted Tomita to fight, not just talk, so he was challenged regularly. Usually, Tomita dealt with the challenges with little problem. However, he suffered defeats in the worst possible venues.

At a demonstration at the US Military Academy at West Point on February 20, 1905, the cadets demanded that Tomita perform, not just talk. Knowing Tomita's limitations as a fighter, especially in this forum, Maeda and Satake tried to dissuade him from asking for volunteers from the audience. Overconfident, Tomita went ahead anyway, with disastrous results. Here is the account, titled "Cadets Down the 'Jap,'" from the February 21, 1905, issue of the *New York Times*:

> West Point, N.Y. Feb 20—In the gymnasium here today the art of Judo had a practical demonstration before the cadet corps and the Academic Board. The board is considering the advisability of adding the Japanese method to the academic curriculum. Prof. Tomet [Tomita], Japan's most famous exponent of the art, and director in the school in Tokio, with his assistant [Maeda] ... gave the exhibition.
>
> The professor wrestled with his assistant throwing him around like a rubber ball. He then called for cadet volunteers. Cadet Tipton, the husky All-American football centre went on the mat and with football methods soon had jiu-jutsu beaten. The big fellow pinned the wiry Jap flat on his back three times without being thrown in the bout. Cadet Daly also threw the professor.

The second terrible public defeat came in 1908, on the White House lawn, in front of President Theodore Roosevelt and a crowd assembled there. Tomita was asked to fight as well as lecture. (Maeda and Satake, who had parted ways with Tomita not long after the West Point debacle in 1905, were not present because they were overseas wrestling in challenge matches. It is unclear who Tomita's assistants were.) Tomita was defeated in a challenge match by a 240-pound football player who got him in a crushing bear hug.

Given these public defeats, Tomita had no chance of making it in the United States and returned to Japan in 1910.

After the disastrous start in America in 1905, it is not certain what else Tomita did during his five-year stay. He taught judo here and there, and held self-defense classes for women. Although Tomita did not look like the type who enjoyed military science, it is said that he studied the American approach to boxing, weight lifting, riflery, and the like. When he returned to Japan, Tomita gave instruction in those subjects at a physical education academy while continuing to teach judo at the Kodokan and at various colleges. Tomita was awarded Kodokan seventh dan upon his death on January 13, 1937.

Tomita's son Tsuneo (1904–67, judo fifth dan) became a famous novelist, primarily writing about the second of the Four Kings, Shiro Saigo. His novel *Sugata Sanshiro*, based on Saigo's life, was published in 1942. The following year a movie of that title directed by Akira Kurosawa (Kurosawa's first film) appeared. Over the following years, six feature films, five TV series, and four manga comic book versions of *Sugata Sanshiro* made Saigo much more of a legend than Kano himself in Japan. Actually, the real story of Saigo's life is far more amazing than any work of fiction.

Shiro Saigo

Nearly everything related to important dates, places, and events in Saigo's life is hazy. The following information is an outline, but there is much more to the story than we will ever know. He was born as Shiro Shida in 1866 in Aizu-Wakamatsu. The father of the household, Teijiro Shida, was an officer in the forces of the Aizu-Wakamatsu Clan, which was on the losing side of the war surrounding the fall of the shogunate and the 1868 restoration of the Emperor Meiji. In the ensuing chaos, the Shida family was forced to evacuate to the Tsugawa District. Shiro lost his father when he was six, and the family circumstances became even

Shiro Saigo (1866–1922).

more strained. The Shida family moved near the Agano River and became shipbuilders and operated ferryboats. Shiro worked as an oarsman, an occupation that partly accounts for the excellent balance he displayed as a martial artist.

As a child, Shiro was said to have been constantly getting into fights, a bad habit he never got over. Shiro entered the local elementary school, Tsugawa Shogakko, when it was established in 1873. (The school signboard had been brushed by Tesshu Yamaoka.) By the age of fourteen, Shiro was acting as an assistant instructor at the school. However, Shiro's dream was to enter a military academy and become a great general. Together with his friend Yojiro Sato, the sixteen-year-old Shiro headed for the capital, Tokyo, in 1882.

However, without much formal education and lacking the proper connections, Shiro found it impossible to enter a military academy. It is said he worked as a rickshaw driver and did other odd jobs to support himself. He also seems to have trained at the Tenjin Shin-yo dojo of Keitaro Inoue, Kano's fellow disciple of Iso. The story goes that because of Shiro's obvious talent, Kano recruited him for the Kodokan. Kano told him, "You can study in my academy, train at the dojo, and have enough to eat." Consequently, ragamuffin Shiro Shida (hereafter Saigo) became the Kodokan's second live-in student.

There is great controversy about Saigo's martial arts training before he entered the Kodokan. Some believe he was an accomplished martial artist, trained in the Daito ryu techniques of the Aizu-Wakamatsu Clan. Others, including some Daito ryu people, maintain that he did not learn any Daito ryu techniques, and even if he did, his training couldn't have been extensive because he was only sixteen years old at the time he entered the Kodokan. He got everything from Kodokan judo. However, the fact of the matter is that Saigo certainly learned martial arts in Aizu-Wakamatsu from somebody. Kano wrote that right from the start, he had a very difficult time handling Saigo.

Since Saigo quickly learned how to counter Kano's every technique, Kano had to constantly refine his techniques in an attempt to stay one step ahead of his pupil. In other words, Kano learned as much from Saigo as Saigo learned from Kano. Kano proudly wrote that when Saigo first entered the Kodokan, he was easy to throw, but thanks to his judo training, he quickly learned how to be more aggressive—indeed, fearless. However, even though Saigo appeared to be easy to throw, he always landed on his feet. Letting his opponent toss him about in the air for ten minutes was likely a ploy. Once the opponent was exhausted from all his efforts, Saigo lowered the boom. That is exactly what happened in the match between Saigo and Terushima (or Kochi).

Further, many people left accounts of Saigo's extraordinary skill with weapons, such as the sword, the spear, and the iron rod—something he could have not picked up at the Kodokan because Kano disliked weapons work. It is true, however, that everyone remarked that Saigo's genius was such that he needed to see a technique only once to remember it—and then often improve it. Saigo was Kodokan fifth dan by age twenty-one, an extremely fast promotion track—he went directly to fifth dan, skipping fourth.

In 1884, two years before the big Tokyo tournament in 1886, Shiro mysteriously returned to Aizu-Wakamatsu to be adopted by Chikanori (aka Tonomo) Hoshina, thus becoming Shiro Hoshina. Chikanori was held to be the grand master of Daito ryu aiki-jutsu. He is supposed to have transmitted that martial art tradition first to Shiro and later to the notorious Sokaku Takeda (or vice versa). No, others claim, there is no proof that Chikanori was an actual martial art master, but that is not so strange given the subterfuge for which the Daito ryu is famous—perhaps Chikanori did not want to let anyone know he was a martial art master, and deliberately misled people into believing that he was merely a mild-mannered Confucian scholar, Shinto priest, and administrator.

After the 1886 Tokyo tournament, Saigo visited Chikanori again, this time to be adopted once more, on this occasion into the grand Saigo family line, which Chikanori had revived. Chikanori pinned his hopes on Shiro to restore the Saigo family line. Thus, Shiro became "Shiro Saigo," the name by which he is known to history. The ancient Saigo family line was one of Japan's most illustrious. In an interview, Sokaku's son Tokimune Takeda stated that Saigo was Chikanori's illegitimate son. (Since Chikanori was even shorter than Saigo—he was said to be only about four-and-a-half feet tall—that might account for Saigo's diminutive frame, and there is a physical resemblance between the two, such a claim is not so far-fetched.) Takeda believed that Chikanori took Saigo in when he was nine years old and taught him Daito ryu techniques. Around the same time, Chikanori was teaching Sokaku as well. Later, when Saigo was at the Kodokan, he introduced Sokaku to

Kano. (The one thing that Chikanori, Sokaku, and Saigo had in common is that all three were tiny men, well under five feet tall.)

Discussing the history of the Saigo family line, Daito ryu ai-ki-jutsu, and the relationship of Chikanori, Shiro, and Sokaku both to the Daito ryu and to one another is beyond the scope of this book, perhaps any book, because these matters are too convoluted, contradictory, and confused to sort out. We will never know the whole story.

As for Saigo's departure from the Kodokan, the Kodokan version is that Saigo was expelled for unspecified reasons, with no mention of his part in engaging in a full-scale brawl. On Saigo's side, he claimed that he voluntarily ran away to join the forces of the *tairiku ronin*, a motley group of Japanese nationals who provided moral and material support for the revolutionary movements in Asia, particularly of Sun Yat-sen in China and Kim Ok-gyun in Korea. The group consisted of agent provocateurs, saboteurs, spies, military men, gunrunners, gangsters, ruffians, opportunists, adventurers, and, perhaps, a few idealists. The revolutionaries in China and Korea needed the support of Japanese right-wing organizations such as the Black Dragon Society, but they were wary—rightly so, as it turned out—of Japanese intentions.

Joining the tairiku ronin was one way for Saigo to fulfill his childhood dream of becoming a great military leader. For the next ten years, it is not clear where and when Saigo visited Asia. It is likely he was active in China, Korea, and Taiwan, but because he was on secret missions, there is no record of any travel. Even though Saigo had supposedly been expelled from the Kodokan, he continued to teach judo in a number of widely scattered places. He opened a dojo in his hometown of Tsugawa in 1892. In 1894, he was in Sendai and may have stayed there for nearly a year serving as the head instructor of the judo club at the Sendai Second Higher School. In 1896, he was in Kyushu acting as head instructor at Chikuma Higher School.

Then, for the next six years, Saigo disappeared. (Disappearing from the scene is a Daito ryu tradition. Sokaku dropped off the radar screen for thirteen years.) This is the period when Saigo probably spent most of his time in Asia.

He next surfaced as editor in chief and war correspondent for the *Toyo Hinode Shimbun*, a far-right newspaper founded by Tengan Suzuki (1867–1926) in Nagasaki in 1902. A number of tairiku ronin had settled in the international port of Nagasaki, and the city was a hotbed of ultranationalist activity. Saigo was an important and influential member of that community. When Sun Yatsen visited Nagasaki in 1913, a commemorative photo was taken at the home of Tengan Suzuki. It is remarkable how small in stature Saigo appears, much shorter than anyone else in the photo. One would never guess that the tiny fellow was one of the all-time greats of the martial arts, East or West.

At the age of forty-six, Saigo finally got married, to the former courtesan Chika Nakagawa, owner of a high-class restaurant where he had been a frequent customer. They had two children, a boy and a girl. Saigo did not settle down much after his marriage. In addition to teaching judo, he had become recognized as a master of kyudo, Japanese archery, and taught that as well. Saigo was supposed to have learned kyudo from a master archer in Nagasaki, but his skill with the bow is another indication that Saigo had practiced that martial art as well when he was young in Aizu-Wakamatsu. Further, he became the first coach of the Nagasaki Swim Club. Of course, Saigo had been a ferryman, so it was natural he was a strong swimmer. However, samurai swimming was part of the martial arts curriculum in Aizu-Wakamatsu. Saigo likely learned how to swim for miles with one arm raised above the water so as to keep a sword dry; spend hours underwater breathing through a tube; and the best way to capsize an enemy boat loaded with soldiers and equipment. Saigo was also said to be a deadly shot with a rifle.

Even in his fifties, Saigo never stopped drinking and fighting. Once on his way home from a night out on the town, Saigo heard a commotion on the bridge ahead. A group of five or six foreign sailors were beating a rickshaw driver. Even though he was drunker than usual, Saigo came to the driver's aid. The burly sailors laughed out loud: "Scram, midget!" Much to their great surprise and considerable pain, in a flash, the pocket Hercules subsequently hurled each of them into the river.

Saigo was undoubtedly delighted that the ruffians were foreigners. Unlike Kano, who was educated largely by Westerners, who had many Western students, and who had friends and acquaintances all over Europe and the United States, Saigo had an intense dislike of Westerners all his life. As a child in Tsugawa, Saigo got in trouble for throwing a rock at the American traveler Isabella Bird, who happened to be visiting the village. As a tairiku ronin, Saigo was dedicated to ridding Asia of the evil Western barbarians, and perhaps eliminated a few personally. In Nagasaki, he was leader of the gang that drove the French missionary priest Michel Sartre out of town.

Once at a carnival in Nagasaki, there was a large, formidable-looking martial arts master, hawking his book *The Secrets of Judo*. He asked anyone from the crowd to come up for a demonstration of the secret powers one can acquire from reading his book. The master was quite skilled and easily threw every challenger, taking care not to hurt them (because then they couldn't buy his book). Since the crowd was impressed after witnessing the master's prowess, he sold many books. Suddenly, a tiny, fifty-year-old gentleman appeared before the master. "Isn't there a stronger challenger present than this little fellow?" the master asked the onlookers. "I'm quite strong," the small gentleman assured him. "Sure you are," the master said with a laugh as he started to grip the gentleman's collar. However, in a flash, the master was flat on his back. "You *are* pretty good," the dazed master said. Without another word, the diminutive challenger stuffed a copy of *The Secrets of Judo* into his bag and scurried off, much to the amusement of the crowd. That tiny gentleman was Saigo.

In 1919, on a visit to Tokyo, Saigo was invited to Kano's home and got to visit with his teacher and many old friends. Saigo died in 1922 at the age of fifty-six. Kano awarded Saigo the posthumous rank of sixth dan. On the certificate, Kano wrote, "Out of the many students I have had, Saigo's technique was the best."

In a way, Saigo was a cofounder of the technical judo element of the Kodokan. The only other person Kano trained with as much is Tomita, who was weaker and considerably less skilled. Kano and Saigo spent hours and hours training together comparing technical notes. It was Saigo, not Kano, who handled all the challengers at the Kodokan and at rival dojos. Kano never trained with any of the other Four Kings the way he did with Saigo.

Sakujiro Yokoyama

The next king is Sakujiro Yokoyama (1864–1912). Yokoyama, of the Tenjin Shin'yo ryu, entered the Kodokan in 1886 after tiny Saigo defeated the much bigger Yokoyama in a challenge match. Thereafter, Saigo and Yokoyama were the keenest of rivals. Their respective approaches were totally opposite. Saigo's judo was described as being like that of an expertly trained thoroughbred; Yokoyama's judo was like that of a wild boar. Saigo used finesse; Yokoyama used power. Saigo's movements were like a finely forged blade; Yokoyama's movements were like a broadsword. (Yokoyama was fierce, to be sure; when he was thirteen years old, he supposedly sliced a burglar in two with a sword.)

Yokoyama was already a master of Tenjin Shin'yo ryu jujutsu, so he was made second dan within his first six months at the Kodokan. Yokoyama was considered the most physically powerful of the Four Kings.

Yokoyama was nicknamed "Demon." He was in the dojo from morning to night, and when he wasn't there, he was outdoors swinging a heavy iron rod. Yokoyama tried to study at the Kano Academy, but he kept falling asleep during class. When Kano asked Yokoyama to read something, he said, "The characters are doing randori, so I can't make them out."

He carried a rope with him as he walked along the road. Whenever he saw a heavy boulder, he put the rope around the stone and flung it over his shoulder with a judo throw. He was what we would call today an "ultra-athlete." He demanded that his disciples train so hard, wear themselves out so completely, that they would never tire when faced with a real challenge match. The following tale is typical. One day, Yokoyama was out with his disciples. When they came across a thick pine tree by the side of the road, Yokoyama commanded, "Throw that pine tree!" Of course, there is no way anyone can throw a pine tree, but Yokoyama made his students grab the trunk and try to apply judo throws. "What kind of weaklings are you! Your attacks are so timid the pine branches are not swaying an inch!" After much fruitless effort, the group continued on their way. Yokoyama made the students walk in front of him. He kicked a student's leg from behind to test if he was walking correctly—if his posture was evenly balanced and he was aware of possible attacks from the rear. At the end of this trying day, Yokoyama told the students, "Wherever you find yourself, you are in a dojo."

Yokoyama's specialty was *tengu-nage* ("mountain-devil throw"), said to be nearly on a par with Saigo's yama-arashi. It is not certain exactly what tengu-nage entailed. The name of the technique may be partly ascribed to Yokoyama's other nickname, "Tengu." Once, Yokoyama was traveling in the rural Hakone area. He met up with some rowdy porters and a fight ensued. Yokoyama thrashed them all so badly that they said to him, "What are you, some kind of tengu?" Yokoyama replied, "Yes, and I will be back if you don't behave yourselves!"

As we have seen, both Saigo and Yokoyama liked street fighting. Although potential assailants were more wary of the much bigger and stronger-looking Yokoyama than Saigo, he still managed to get into plenty of brawls, usually against a group of attackers—no one would dare to challenge Yokoyama man-to-man. In a well-known story, Yokoyama and the young Mifune battered a group of twelve or thirteen scoundrels who had attacked them in a restaurant. Yokoyama was suspended a couple of times from the Kodokan because of his rough behavior outside the dojo.

Yokoyama and Eisuke Oshima wrote one of the first Kodokan training manuals, *Judo Kyohan*. It was translated into English and published in 1915. The book illustrates judo in the old style—plenty of pins, locks, and chokes.

During the period of the Russo-Japanese War of 1904–5, the

"Food Bandit" incident occurred at the Kodokan. For several nights running, an intruder broke into the Kodokan and pilfered the food supplies of the live-in trainees. Two students were posted as guards, but when they encountered the bandit, who was decked out in Chinese ninja-like garb, they were severely beaten. After thrashing the pair, the bandit sneered, "You pathetic weaklings! Don't you have anyone better to put on guard?" Upon receiving a report of that night's alarming event, the senior members of the dojo were nonplussed. If it took four or five Kodokan men to subdue a single bandit, it would make their judo look bad. So they asked Yokoyama to defend the honor of the Kodokan. Naturally, there are two versions of what occurred:

1. That night, as anticipated, the bandit dropped from the ceiling and an epic battle ensued. The Chinese boxer was very skilled, but Yokoyama held his own with his judo techniques. Yokoyama eventually blocked a kick and immediately applied a judo throw; the boxer went down but simultaneously struck a sharp blow with his left-hand sword to Yokoyama's side, thus making it a draw.
2. Yokoyama defeated the boxer with a clean throw and pin. The boxer got up and said, "Thank you. I've learned a lot."

The Chinese boxer was actually an Okinawan Shorei ryu karate master fighter named Gisho Matsumura. Since Matsumura wanted to see how really good his karate was, he camouflaged himself in Chinese kung fu garb and went to the Japanese mainland to challenge various martial artists, often in unexpected circumstances such as pretending he was a burglar. As Matsumura soundly defeated the lower-ranked Kodokan men, he returned for a real fight against an instructor. Whatever the outcome was, it is likely that Matsumura did in fact thank Yokoyama. Either way, Matsumura felt he honed his fighting prowess.

Yokoyama enjoyed relating these two samurai tales to his students:

Prior to the Meiji Restoration in 1868, certain samurai went swaggering around town wearing two swords, long and short. These samurai deliberately started fights by running into a person, making him touch the samurai's sword, an unpardonable sin that had to be avenged. The samurai would then cut down the hapless victim, much of the time simply to test the cutting quality of his blade. Once, three samurai were in town to make trouble and they confronted a *ronin* (wandering masterless samurai), charging him for not showing enough respect. The preening samurai were finely turned out in expensive kimonos, and carrying high-quality swords. In contrast, the ronin was shabbily dressed in a threadbare robe, and the scabbard of his sword was badly worn. The ronin remained calm and would not back down. The bullying samurai surrounded the ronin and rushed in to attack. In a flash, the ronin cut down two of the samurai. After seeing what had transpired, the third ran away. Yokoyama's moral was: "Never judge a book by its cover."

The second tale is that one night when Yokoyama was returning home, he witnessed an altercation between a young rickshaw driver and an elderly man, whom Yokoyama surmised was probably in his seventies. Upon dropping the older gentleman off, the tough rickshaw driver demanded more money, threatening to beat his customer. Yokoyama moved in to come the old man's aid. Suddenly, however, the old man threw the ruffian and pinned him solidly on the street. The lock was so powerful that the rickshaw driver could not use his arms after the old fellow let him up. Yokoyama's moral in this case: "Never judge a book by its cover, and never stop being a martial artist regardless of your age." (It is not beyond the realm of possibility that the old man was Sokaku Takeda, who was notorious for doing such things, even in his final years.)

Yokoyama was a heavy drinker, even for a Japanese martial artist, who typically drink like fish. After Yokoyama and Kano had a falling-out—among other things, Yokoyama thought that he, not Kano, should be in charge of the technical side of judo—Yokoyama hardly taught or trained at all in his forties. He developed cancer of the esophagus and died in 1912 at the young age of forty-nine. Yokoyama was awarded the first Kodokan eighth dan upon his death.

Yoshitsugu Yamashita

The last of the Four Kings was Yoshitsugu (aka Yoshiaki) Yamashita (1865–1935), who entered the Kodokan in 1884. Yamashita belonged to a samurai family originally from Kanazawa. When Kano was a college student, he lived in the same Tokyo neighborhood as Yamashita, and they played catch sometimes. (Both of them liked baseball.) Yamashita was well versed in the martial arts of the Toshin ryu and Tenjin Shin'yo ryu before he entered the Kodokan. (Yamashita was Kano's partner whenever he demonstrated the old-style jujutsu forms.) Yamashita's rise through the Kodokan ranks was rapid: he was fourth dan in two years. At first, Yamashita relied much more on power and crushing techniques in jujutsu style rather than the more flexible and less dangerous Kodokan judo.

Like Saigo and Yokoyama, Yamashita was a street fighter. Yamashita relished thrashing his thuggish attackers, maiming or reportedly even killing several of them. For that kind of mayhem, Yamashita was arrested. He successfully pleaded self-defense, but the Kodokan suspended Yamashita for "excessive use of force," also like Saigo and Yokoyama. (Of the Four Kings, Tomita was the only one who didn't engage in street fights; perhaps that is why he was not so good at handling challenges.)

Yamashita formally causing a lot of grief to people both inside and outside of the Kodokan. It was obvious that he wanted to have a go at it with Kano himself. Kano disarmed him: "Yamashita, you are strong, but you delight in injuring your partners. If you act like that, sooner or later, you are going to get injured yourself. It will come back to you. It is up to you to make the decision: 'Will I use my judo to kill, or to give life?'" Yamashita changed dramatically after that.

Yamashita formally introduced Kodokan judo to the United States. After seeing judo on a business trip to Japan, Samuel Hill, a railroad executive, impetuously decided that his nine-year-old son—whom the workaholic Hill realized he was neglecting—should learn judo to build both his body and his confidence. After some negotiating, the English-speaking Yamashita was invited, at

Hill's expense, to the United States. Yamashita brought his wife, Fude, who was also a skilled judo practitioner, and a judo student named Saburo Kawaguchi as an assistant. They arrived in Seattle in September 1903.

Yamashita and Kawaguchi held several demonstrations in Seattle. Naturally, onlookers wanted proof that judo worked. Yamashita settled the matter by deftly handling a two-hundred-pound boxer. Mr. and Mrs. Yamashita then went to Washington, D.C., to teach judo. Most of their students were from the upper levels of society, primarily young women. The training was genteel, a world away from the rough-and-tumble dojos of Japan.

In 1904, Yamashita and Fude were introduced to President Theodore Roosevelt by Isamu Takeshita, the Japanese naval attaché. (Takeshita played a seminal role in promoting both judo and especially aikido at home and abroad.) Roosevelt was a fan of Western fighting arts such as wrestling and boxing, and had had some lessons previously in jujutsu. As mentioned, Okakura's patron and Roosevelt's close friend William Sturgis Bigelow impressed Roosevelt with the effectiveness of jujutsu by pinning Secretary of War Elihu Root. Bigelow arranged for John J. O'Brian to give Roosevelt formal lessons in jujutsu. When O'Brian was stationed in Nagasaki as a police superintendent, he learned non-Kodokan jujutsu from a teacher named Kishoku Inoue. O'Brian instructed Roosevelt in March and April 1902. Bigelow sent Roosevelt six judo uniforms and a book on judo (which one is not specified). In 1904, after seeing Yamashita's Kodokan-style judo, Roosevelt asked Yamashita to teach judo at the White House to him, some family members, and a few staff members.

"The Register of Professor Y. Yamada" states:

> We, the undersigned, appearing before the professor, Yoshitsugu Yamashita, being duly sworn upon our oath, declare that we become his pupils and agree to allegiance and fidelity to the honor and respect of the art of judo and all the teachings of the professor.

On that page of the register, we find the signatures of Theodore Roosevelt, Oliver H. P. La Farge I (architect and uncle of the writer Oliver H. P. La Farge II), Gifford Pinchot (later to become first chief of the United States Forest Service), Admiral Takeshita, and a dozen others, including three children aged nine and one aged twelve.

Roosevelt's practice of judo was in the Rough Rider mode, much more enthusiastic than well planned, so Yamashita had to exercise caution when he threw the president of the United States on his ass. ("The harder the attack, the harder the fall.")

In 1905, Yamashita got a plum job at the US Naval Academy at Annapolis. There were only about twenty-five students in the class, and reaction to the Kodokan judo manner of teaching was mixed—some students thought it too rigid and "Oriental." Yamashita was let go at the end of the term, but President Roosevelt interceded with the secretary of the navy to keep him on for a second term. However, when the second term was up, Yamashita was not rehired. Roosevelt once again interceded, but both the academy and Yamashita had had enough. In preference to Yamashita, the academy hired Tom Jenkins, a semiretired professional wrestler. Jenkins taught at the academy for thirty-six years.

Yamashita's career in the United States was checkered. While Yamashita performed better in challenge matches than Tomita did later, Yamashita's performance in some of the matches—a couple could have been considered draws—failed to impress the onlookers, especially military audiences. The military saw little value in the practice of judo for men in service, one reason perhaps being that it took so long to master. Punching, kicking, and wrestling were much easier to learn and more practical to apply.

Even Roosevelt, in a letter to his son Kirmit dated February 24, 1905, expressed doubts that judo fighters could hold their own once the much bigger and stronger American wrestlers or boxers caught on to the judo tricks.

I still box with Grant, who has now become the champion middleweight wrestler of the United States. Yesterday we had Professor Yamashita up here to wrestle with Grant. It was very interesting, but of course jiu jitsu and our wrestling are so far apart that it is difficult to make any comparison between them. Wrestling is simply a sport with rules almost as conventional as those of tennis, while jiu jitsu is really meant for practice in killing or disabling our adversary. In consequence, Grant did not know what to do except to put Yamashita on his back, and Yamashita was perfectly content to be on his back. Inside of a minute Yamashita had choked Grant, and inside two minutes he got an elbow hold on him that would have enabled him to break his arm; so there is no question that he could have put Grant out. So far this made it evident the jiu jitsu man could handle the ordinary wrestler. But Grant, in the actual wrestling and throwing was about as good as the Japanese and he was so much stronger that he evidently hurt and wore out the Japanese. With a little practice in the art I am sure that one of our big wrestlers or boxers, simply because of greatly superior strength, would be able to kill any of those Japanese, who though very good men for their inches and pounds are altogether too small to hold their own against big, powerful, quick men who are as well trained. (From *Theodore Roosevelt's Letters to His Children*, published in 1919)

After such criticism, the disappointed Yamashita and his wife returned to Japan in mid-1906.

(Regarding the visits of Yamashita and Tomita to the United States, one thing is puzzling. Since Tomita was in the United States from early 1905, and Yamashita left in 1906, the pair were in the country together for over a year. It is highly unlikely that Yamashita did not know that Tomita was there, or vice versa, but the two seemed not to have worked together, or even acknowledged each other, perhaps being at cross-purposes. It could be that while Yamashita was in America by private invitation, Tomita was there as an official delegate of the Kodokan, and they were on separate missions. The relationship between

Yamashita and Tomita when they were both in the United States is rather murky.)

Back in Japan, Yamashita taught at various colleges and the police academy. Yamashita died in 1935 and was posthumously awarded the Kodokan's first tenth dan by Kano.

Here are Yamashita's "Dos and Don'ts for Learning Judo":

1. Win with technique, not brute force.
2. The best defense is a good offense.
3. Learn how to take breakfalls. Good breakfalls will make all your techniques better.
4. Practice moving in all directions, over and over, while staying centered.
5. Train and train, in practice and in contests. (Yamashita was famed for trying to engage in ten thousand contests in a year.)
6. Train with everyone. Don't pick and choose your partners.
7. Refine your techniques based on actual practice, not theory.
8. Train with all your body and mind.
9. Listen to your instructors.
10. Don't do anything halfway.
11. Observe how others perform the techniques well.
12. Don't overeat or overdrink.
13. Never get overconfident.
14. Learning in judo never stops.

Other Prominent Japanese Students
Itsuro Munakata

One of the earliest students at the Kodokan was Itsuro Munakata (1866–1941). He entered the Kodokan and the Kano Academy in February 1884. Two years later, the disciplined Munakata became the student leader of the Kano Academy. Munakata was studious and went on to have a long career as an educator, serving as headmaster or principal at a number of higher schools, all the while promoting both book learning and judo. Munakata was a teacher after Kano's own heart, a staunch Confucian scholar who emphasized

The dashing and heroic naval officer Takeo Hirose (1868–1904), who died in the Russo-Japanese War. Kano posthumously promoted Hirose to sixth dan, the highest rank at the time. Tragically, the love of Hirose's life was Russian, Ariadna Kowalsky.

equally the physical and spiritual dimensions of judo. Munakata authored the textbook *Judo* in 1913, with a preface by Kano.

Takeo Hirose

Navy commander Takeo Hirose was mentioned earlier as being one of the first generation of Kodokan trainees, entering in 1889. Since Hirose was a student at the Naval Academy, he could only train at the dojo on Sunday. He was there from first thing in the morning until closing at night, skipping lunch to practice nonstop. When it snowed, he removed his *geta* (wooden clogs) and walked to the dojo in order to toughen his feet to the cold. At the Red and White Teams Tournament in 1890, Hirose was the first competitor in Kodokan history to defeat five men in a row, thus earning immediate promotion to the next dan (in his case, second dan). Hirose drew with the sixth man he faced, Shigoro Baba, said to be nearly as talented as Saigo. (Unfortunately, Baba was part of Saigo's gang that was constantly provoking street fights, including in the red-light district. Baba's fighting motto was "70 percent atemi, 30 percent throws." Reportedly,

Baba killed a gangster, and, like Saigo, Baba was expelled for dishonoring the Kodokan.)

Hirose often made social calls on Demon Yokoyama, bringing gifts of whiskey and sweet cakes. Hirose did not drink, but he knew Yokoyama loved it. Hirose loved cakes, so he got to eat his own presents. The two had many spirited conversations about judo during these visits, typically resulting in impromptu instruction sessions in the living room. Yokoyama later said, "I could handle Hirose in the dojo, but he really pressed me in my living room."

In 1897, Hirose was sent to Russia to serve as a military attaché. During his nearly five years there, he impressed the Russians with his judo skills against challenges by wrestlers, but evidently did not teach judo. Hirose was quite found of the Russians, and had a beautiful Russian girlfriend, perhaps fiancée, named Ariadna Kowalsky. The outbreak of the Russo-Japanese War was terribly hard for Hirose to bear. He was sworn to duty, however. Hirose died at sea during the Battle of Ryojun Bay while trying to rescue the pilot of his sinking ship. Ariadna was devastated when she heard of his death and immediately put on mourning dress. The love affair between Hirose and Ariadna is widely known in Japan these days thanks to the sad story being featured in the popular NHK historical drama *Saka no ue no kumo* (Clouds above the hills).

Hirose's fellow Kodokan trainee Yuasa had also become a naval commander, and he too perished within a few months of Hirose in the sea battles of the Russo-Japanese War. Sensing that he and Hirose would never return, Yuasa had written Kano a farewell letter expressing gratitude for all that Kano had taught them. Takejiro Yuasa and Takeo Hirose were enshrined as "War Gods" by the navy, and promoted posthumously to sixth dan Kodokan judo by Kano. In the Kano Jigoro Memorial Hall at the Kodokan, large photos of Hirose and Yuasa frame the central display area with a painting of Kano in the middle.

Reijiro Wakatsuki

The "Pacifist Prime Minister" Reijiro Wakatsuki (1866–1949) entered the Kodokan the same year as Hirose. Wakatsuki, born in

Shimane, came from an extremely poor background and had to work as a wood gather and houseboy to subsist when he was young. Wakatsuki needed to borrow money to make it to Tokyo for the Tokyo University entrance exam. He graduated at the top of his class, with a grade average of 98.5. Wakatsuki went to the Kodokan every day after class to practice judo. He obtained second dan, and was said to have been quite skillful at throws, particularly seio-nage.

Upon graduation, Wakatsuki entered government service, and eventually became a cabinet minister and then prime minister. First as home minister and then as prime minister from 1926 to 1927 and in 1931, Wakatsuki worked tirelessly to enact the Universal Manhood Suffrage Law and the Peace Preservation Law, and to secure ratification of the international disarmament treaty. The military and ultranationalists hated Wakatsuki for championing such peace activities. He condemned the Kwantung Army in China as no longer a Japanese army because they did not obey the Japanese government and acted as an independent force. Unfortunately, try as he might, as prime minister Wakatsuki was unable to rein in the military. Wakatsuki opposed both the Sino-Japanese War and war with the United States. When the war with the United States did start, Wakatsuki publicly tried to get the conflict stopped as soon as possible. Wakatsuki spent the war in troubled retirement, emerging in 1945 to urge Prime Minister Kentaro Suzuki to accept surrender to save the nation from further destruction. Wakatsuki was a prosecution witness at the International Military Tribunal for the Far East.

While Wakatsuki enjoyed alcohol throughout his life, he had the ability to get drunk but then instantly turn stone-cold sober if an important matter of state came up. After the matter was taken care of, Wakatsuki would go back to being drunk.

Koki Hirota

Koki Hirota (1878–1948) was the other Kano student who became prime minister. Although Hirota attempted to be as much of a peacemaker as Wakatsuki, he was executed as a class A war criminal, a judgment considered by many a great injustice.

Prime Minister Koki Hirota (1878–1948), "the man who devoted his life to preventing war condemned as a war criminal."

Hirota was born in Fukuoka, the son of a stonemason. The family was so poor that Hirota had to work his way through primary school by taking odd jobs around the neighborhood. Even as a child, his calligraphy was so good that he brushed inscriptions for his father to carve on tombstones. One piece, "Tenman-gu," was posted on the local shrine of that name. Hirota was eight years old at the time. He never missed a day of school in his entire life. Hirota had started judo in his hometown, and continued to train at the Kodokan when he was a college student in Tokyo. Hirota was extraordinarily skilled at judo (with the rank of second dan) and could have gone on to be a professional instructor. However, Hirota had his sights set on becoming a diplomat.

In 1923, Hirota got his wish and entered the Ministry of Foreign Affairs. Hirota's approach to diplomacy was "slow and sure." He held a number of foreign posts, eventually serving as ambassador to the Netherlands and the Soviet Union. Every morning throughout his life, Hirota did what his family called his "judo dance." (This was his own version of the *seiryoku zenyo kokumin taiku* Kodokan exercises. Hirota executed some of them as if he were fighting with a partner, so in a sense Hirota had a judo match every day.) Every evening he read the *Analects* of Confucius. A few times during his career, he was forced to assume a judo stance to face down aggressive opponents in the government or foreign reporters. Hirota never forgot his humble roots and lived simply, eating a bowl of noodles every day for lunch. He and his wife hated putting on airs, dressing up, and attending diplomatic social events. Hirota's colleagues referred to their "villa" in Kamukura as the "shack."

In 1933, the quiet, hardworking Hirota become foreign minister. The US ambassador Joseph Grew praised Hirota as the one official in the government genuinely committed to peace. In his diary, Grew wrote, "For me, there are no finer people in the world than the best type of Japanese. I am rather inclined to place Hirota among them; if he could have his way unhampered by the military I believe that he would steer the country into safer and saner channels." Hirota was profiled in a May 21, 1934, *Time* magazine cover article entitled "Keeper of the Peace," in which Hirota declared, "There will be no war as long as I am Foreign Minister." Later, in the March 25, 1936, issue of the *New York Times*, Hirota made the same pledge, only this time as prime minister: "There will be no war as long as I am Prime Minister." (Hirota served as prime minister from March 9, 1936, to February 2, 1937.)

After resigning as prime minister, the capable Hirota was quickly reappointed foreign minister. As ever, Hirota opposed the military, but there was a limit to what he could do, and thus he had to play ball with the armed forces. The army ignored Hirota's entreaties to seek a truce in China. On December 13, 1937, the Japanese army entered Nanking. During the ensuing "Nanking massacre," certain rogue Japanese divisions ran amok, killing, looting, and raping despite strict orders from the commanding general, Iwane Matsui, that his troops protect and take care of Chinese officials and citizens. Hirota exploded in anger and dismay when he got news of the atrocities and demanded that the army take immediate steps to impose discipline and treat all Chinese citizens properly.

When General Matsui, who had been ill and thus was not present during the first few days of the invasion, found out what had happened, he was appalled. On February 4, 1938, Matsui held a public memorial service in Nanking for both the Chinese and Japanese war dead. Offering his apologies and sympathies to the Chinese victims, Matsui berated his troops about the reports of atrocities he had heard. He denounced such soldiers as being unworthy of service in the Imperial Army. From now on, every soldier was to keep strict military discipline and refrain from harming innocent citizens. Matsui never recovered from the shame of what his soldiers had done.

Despite the fact that both Hirota and Matsui behaved as well as could possibly be expected under the circumstances, and that there was no systematic master plan to pillage Nanking (junior officers were the real villains, and the extent and nature of the massacres has been disputed, not only by Japanese denialists but by Western researchers), both were later charged as class A war criminals by the International Military Tribunal for the Far East for their role in the Nanking massacre. As commanding officer in the field, Matsui was ultimately responsible for what happened in Nanking, even if it "wasn't my fault that the troops ignored my commands." However, Hirota, a civilian in Tokyo, had absolutely no power to either curb the troops or court-martial the entire army. Hirota was also accused of the trumped-up charge of consorting with Mitsuru Toyama and his Genyosha terrorist group. Nearly everyone in the Japanese government could have been accused of that.

After the war, when his bitter foes, leaders of the army and navy, saw Hirota in custody with them, they were shocked: "What are you doing here?" Ironically, Hirota, who had clearly spent his entire tenure as foreign and prime minster attempting to make peace, was now being charged as a war criminal. For some difficult-to-fathom reason, Hirota refused to defend himself. It was almost as if Hirota did take responsibility for his actions—he had not done enough to keep his country out of war as foreign and prime minster. Hirota's lawyers had a hard time even convincing him to make a perfunctory plea of "not guilty." He was found guilty and sentenced to hang, the only civilian to be so condemned. (Although fascist prime minister Kiichiro Hiranuma, mentioned above, fanatically condoned all of the Japanese military's wartime behavior and opposed Japan's surrender, believing that every man, woman, and child should fight to the end, he was given life in prison.) In the eyes of many people, including Chief Prosecutor Joseph Keenan, Hirota was the least deserving of that punishment. One hundred thousand people signed a petition to have Hirota's death sentence commuted and submitted it to General Douglas MacArthur—to no avail.

In so many ways, Hirota's life was tragic. One of his sons had committed suicide when he failed his university entrance exams. After a lifetime fighting for peace, Hirota found himself facing execution as a war criminal. His beloved wife, Shizuko, unable to face living without her husband, committed suicide while Hirota was in prison. Hirota faced his scheduled execution with equanimity. He even had a sense of gallows humor. "I have been strangled many times during judo practice. It wasn't so bad."

Hirota went to his death calmly, refusing to join the two condemned prisoners with him—Seishiro Itagaki and Heitaro Kimura—in three cries of *Banzai!* ("Long live the emperor!") before they entered the death chamber.

Ryohei Uchida

A much different type than either Wakatsuki or Hirota was Ryohei Uchida (1874–1937), by far the most infamous member of the Kodokan. Uchida was the chief disciple of Mitsuru Toyama, ultranationalist founder of the Dark Ocean Society (Genyosha), and creator of his own sinister Black Dragon Society (Kokuryukai). Working in conjunction with other ultranationalists, the two groups were notorious for creating chaos and mayhem in Russia, Manchuria, China, and Korea.

Uchida's father, Ryogoro, was a prominent martial artist of the Edo period, so Uchida trained in bojutsu, jujutsu, kenjutsu, and *kyujutsu* from an early age. Uchida was also said to be good at sumo. Uchida entered the Kodokan in 1892. As mentioned,

Uchida was already a skilled martial artist, and he quickly earned the nickname "Killer." Uchida tried not only to defeat but to destroy his opponents. He earned first dan in 1894 and second dan a short time later. During this period, Uchida traveled back and forth to his hometown of Fukuoka to teach at the Tenshin Dojo established there. Uchida also went around challenging and defeating all the other martial arts instructors in the town.

In 1896, Uchida, who had studied the Russian language in college, went to Vladivostok and opened a dojo on the grounds of the Higashi Hongan-ji Mission there. The dojo was in fact a front for Uchida's espionage activities. In 1898, Uchida went to Saint Petersburg, ostensibly as a businessman, but in fact as a spy and agent provocateur. He taught judo at the Japanese consulate. In 1899, Uchida defeated Russia's top wrestler in a mixed martial arts challenge match fought before Czar Nicholas II.

By 1900, Uchida was back in Japan, where he received his fourth dan at the Kodokan. He acted as the judo instructor at Keio University from 1904 to 1906.

In 1906, Uchida returned to East Asia, continuing his nefarious activities and, sadly, using Kodokan judo dojos as his base for espionage. Uchida first established a Kodokan dojo in Seoul, Korea. It is safe to say that Uchida was not teaching the Kodokan judo of Kano, but his own mixture of the Uchida ryu system of weapons and lethal jujutsu techniques, with perhaps a few Kodokan judo throws added. Also, it seems that Uchida was not in his dojo much, spending most of his time engaged in mischief making of the grimmest kind.

It is difficult to determine how much Kano knew about Uchida's activities. Uchida did not practice a great deal at the Kodokan headquarters; he mostly trained at outlying dojos far away from Tokyo, or from Japan itself. Uchida was in close contact with a few senior Kodokan instructors, however, and tried to secretly recruit a few of them to join his Black Dragon Society, founded in 1901. We presume that Kano had little knowledge of what Uchida was actually doing, nor did he approve of it—after all, Uchida was a spy trying to keep his activities hidden—but there is at least one photograph of Kano standing with Uchida. (There is also a photograph of Uchida with Sun Yat-sen.) Uchida did teach under the Kodokan banner. We will likely never find out what the real relationship was (if any) between Kano and Uchida.

Masujiro Honda

A much more positive personality was Masujiro Honda (1866–1925). When Honda entered the Kano Academy and the Kodokan in 1883, Kano told him, "When you study, it is not for getting a good job or making money; study is for improving yourself and benefiting society. When you train in the dojo, it is not for polishing your techniques; it is for polishing your body and spirit. I don't want a student who spends all his time in the library, nor do I want a student who spends all his time in the dojo. I want a student who divides his time between the library and the dojo."

Honda was an excellent student and accomplished judo man, reaching third dan. However, while Kano was in Europe in 1889, Honda became a fervent Christian. As mentioned, Kano did not like religion of any kind, so he expelled Honda from the academy, lest he contaminate the others. However, once Honda was out of the academy, Kano was fine with Honda, in fact recommending him for a position as a teacher at the school in Kumamoto where Kano had been appointed principal. Thereafter, they worked together on a number of projects, Honda writing articles for Kano's journals and Kano writing prefaces for Honda's books.

Honda had an interesting career. Perhaps the best English speaker and writer in the country, Honda was visiting professor or principal at several colleges, an interpreter for visiting dignitaries from abroad and important Japanese diplomats when they traveled overseas, a delegate himself at international conferences, founder of the journal *The Oriental Review* when he was living in New York, and back home editor of the *Japan Times* newspaper. He wrote several books, translated a number of books into Japanese (including *Black Beauty* and *Thoughts on Ethics Selected from the Writings of John Ruskin*), and wrote articles for many overseas publications. Honda was also instrumental in the founding of Japan's first hospital for suffers of Hansen's disease (leprosy) in 1895.

Mitsuyo Maeda

Colorful Mitsuyo Maeda (1878–1941) had a life nearly as fantastic as Shiro Saigo on a much wider international stage. Maeda, then a student at Waseda University, entered the Kodokan in 1895. His teacher was the even-tempered Tomita. Like Saigo, however, Maeda was a fighter. He enjoyed battling everyone, whether in the dojo or in the street. He treated everyone the same—like an enemy. Maeda cut beginners no slack.

As mentioned, Maeda accompanied his teacher Tomita to the United States at the end of 1904, but their demonstrations did not go very well. Tomita was defeated in a big public demonstration at West Point, and even the young bull Maeda reportedly lost at least one challenge match himself at the New York Athletic Club on March 8, 1905. Abashed by the poor performances of Tomita and himself, Maeda became determined to salvage the reputation of Japanese judo.

Tomita and Maeda parted ways at the end of 1905. Since Maeda was a graduate of Waseda, one of the major universities in Japan, he could certainly have made a comfortable living doing something else. However, fighting was Maeda's first and only love. Maeda embarked on a full-time career as professional fighter.

For the next three decades, Maeda (his stage name was Conde Koma, "Count Trouble") fought thousands of battles against every manner of professional and amateur wrestler and boxer, other Japanese judo and jujutsu men, savate exponents, local toughs, and barroom brawlers in every kind of venue imaginable—tournaments, boxing rings, wrestling mats, theaters, music halls, circuses, and bars. Maeda crossed the globe fighting: the United States, the United Kingdom, Spain, Portugal, Belgium, France, Cuba, Mexico, and most important, South America. Unlike today's pampered mixed martial artists who fight once or twice a year, Maeda had at least one match nearly every day for months on end. Over the years, Maeda lost only a handful of matches, so he was able to maintain his reputation as a fighter for decades. Maeda spent his last years mostly in Brazil. Maeda is best known today as being the teacher of Carlos Gracie. Carlos passed on Maeda's unsurpassed knowledge of fighting techniques based on years of hand-to-hand combat to his brothers. From that transmission, the effective fighting system Gracie jujutsu came into being.

Maeda (like many of Kano's other students) considered classic Kodokan judo too tame. Kano's aim was to make Kodokan judo safe for its practitioners, to enable trainees to take breakfalls rather than be thrown headfirst to the ground and to avoid suffering permanent injury caused by forced locks and pins. This meant eliminating the most dangerous techniques. However, it was exactly those techniques that were most effective. As soon as Maeda engaged in mixed matches, he discovered that orthodox Kodokan judo would never work completely against competent Western wrestlers and boxers. In short, Maeda became a mixed martial arts genius, honing his skills by incorporating techniques taken from many fighting systems, albeit primarily based on Kosen judo.

Throughout all this combat showmanship, however, Maeda continued to teach orthodox Kodokan judo and establish regular dojos in various countries. Although Maeda's career as a professional fighter seems to contradict everything a Kodokan judo instructor is supposed to embody, nonetheless, the Kodokan acknowledged Maeda's achievements in spreading judo around the world by awarding him the ranks of sixth dan (1929) and seventh dan (1941, posthumously). Maeda's last words were said to have been, "Hey, bring me my judo uniform."

Hajime Isogai

Hajime Isogai (1871–1947) entered the Kodokan in October 1891, when Kano was teaching in Kumamoto. (He had wanted to enter the Naval Academy but did not meet the height requirement.) When Kano returned to the Kodokan, the senior students reported on Isogai's rapid progress. Isogai was a little cocky. Although Kano rarely engaged in randori with students at the time—he tended to tire out quickly—he had a round with Isogai. Isogai was thrown easily. Isogai was amazed at how fast and precise Kano's movements were.

Isogai, who attained sixth dan by 1904, was one of Kano's chief advisers on the technical aspect of Kodokan judo, especially on the incorporation of jujutsu groundwork into judo. Isogai spent most of his life promoting Kodokan judo in the Kansai area, acting as the head instructor of several colleges and an adviser to martial art organizations in Kyoto. Isogai was considered to be the expert on groundwork (he was the first Kodokan fighter to draw, not lose, to Master Tanabe of the Fusen ryu). An excellent instructor and administrator, Isogai was awarded tenth dan in 1937.

Kunisaburo Iizuka

Kunisaburo Iizuka (1875–1958) entered the Kodokan two months after Isogai, in December 1891. (He was just tall enough to gain admittance to the Naval Academy but then got thrown out for arguing with the principal.) His first teacher was Demon Yokoyama. When Iizuka was third dan, he was invited to teach at his former high school in Kagoshima by the principal, Iwasaki. Kano told Iwasaki, "No, that is a bad idea. He is much too young and immature. [Iizuka was twenty-two at the time.] Kagoshima is too far from Tokyo for me to keep an eye on him and give him guidance." Iwasaki insisted that everything would be fine. Kano finally acceded to Iwasaki's request—nonetheless indicating by his expression "You'll be sorry"—and off Iizuka went to Kagoshima to assume his post as a well-paid judo instructor. Although he could naturally throw the students around the dojo, they did not respect him: "He is as young as we are, smaller in size, and not as smart."

Sure enough, Iizuka lost his temper one night when the students were having a party and injured a couple of them. He was fired. Iizuka returned to the Kodokan, too ashamed to face Kano, and resumed training in a corner of the dojo. Not at all surprised when he found out that Iizuka was back, Kano called the young man into his office. Kano said nothing about what had happened in Kagoshima; he knew that Iizuka had learned his lesson. "You can stay at the Kano Academy for the time being, and come to the Tokyo Teacher Training College twice a week to assist me." In other words, "I will teach you how to be a good instructor."

After that, Iizuka spent his early career as a judo instructor in Fukuoka, in southern Japan. Of all the Kodokan instructors, Iizuka had the closest relationship with Uchida, who was always trying to get Iizuka to become an active member of the Black Dragon Society and aid him in his plots. Iizuka did some work as an agent of the Black Dragon Society in Manchuria for a few months when he was teaching there. (Incidentally, while there are dozens of accounts of judo fighters going against jujutsu men, boxers, and wrestlers, there are not many describing challenge matches against Chinese kung fu boxers, Korean wrestlers, and other Asian martial art systems. Iizuka mentions one such contest in Manchuria. Three groups—judo, kung fu, and Korean wrestlers—each did an exhibition. After that, there were supposed to be challenge matches among the three groups. The Korean wrestlers declined to participate, likely because they realized they were vulnerable to judo groundwork, as they did not have groundwork in their system. The kung fu fighters came up against the judo men, but were, Iizuka reports, soundly defeated.)

Incidentally, two of Iizuka's students in Fukuoka, Seigo Nakano (1886–1943) and Ikkan Miyagawa (1885–1944), did fall completely under the evil influence of Uchida and became prominent figures in the ultranationalist movement in the 1920s and 1930s. Nakano and Miyagawa were the fiercest of judo rivals; in fact, they hated each other. In 1904, in perhaps the most famous grudge match in judo history, Miyagawa defeated Nakano with a throw that was described as being like "cherry blossoms in full bloom." Nakano trained so recklessly in judo that he broke his leg in practice. It never healed properly, and eventually the leg had to be amputated. Nakano was the leader of the fascist movement and a bitter opponent of Hideki Tojo. After Nakano was placed under house arrest in 1943, he committed seppuku in protest. Miyagawa became a professional judo instructor (eventually reaching seventh dan) as well as a leading member of Toyama's Dark Ocean Society. In 1928, Miyagawa won the Fukuoka District seat in the Diet. Miyagawa died in 1944, just before the war ended.

In 1906, Uchida asked Iizuka to take over as judo instructor at Keio University. "I am never there," Uchida told him. "I am too busy with my scheming." Iizuka served as judo instructor at his alma mater, Keio, for thirty-eight years. Even though Kano treated Iizuka kindly after the young man's disastrous start as a judo instructor in Kagoshima, mentioned above, Iizuka was one of the Kodokan instructors who called for Kano's resignation over the arrest of Kano's son Riho as a left-wing sympathizer, and he also threatened to form a rival judo organization. An uneasy truce ensued between Kano and Iizuka. When Iizuka opened his own dojo, the Shigokan, in 1935, Kano did not show up at the ceremony, canceling at the last moment because of "urgent business."

An interesting story is told about Iizuka and Nakano. Iizuka, like many martial art teachers, claimed that night or day he never permitted an opening in his defenses so it would be impossible for anyone to successfully attack him. Upon hearing this, Nakano decided to try to catch Iizuka off guard. Nakano followed Iizuka home one night, sneaked up on him, and whacked his teacher sharply across the back of his leg with a bamboo sword. Although startled, Iizuka retained his composure and, without missing a beat, came up with this excuse: "I knew you were only armed with a bamboo sword, so I let you hit me. If it had been a live blade, I would have evaded the attack."

Once, Iizuka was serving as judge at a judo match. The larger competitor used his weight advantage to score a point on the smaller competitor early in the contest, and then spent the rest of the match protecting his lead by evasion. At the end of the contest, Iizuka awarded the match to the smaller competitor, to everyone's surprise. When asked the reason for such a decision, Iizuka replied, "The bigger man spent most of the match running away. The smaller competitor never gave up trying. That is the Kodokan spirit." The other judges in the Kodokan complained to Kano that Iizuka was not following the rules, and should not be acting as a judge in matches. "No," Kano said, "Iizuka is the kind of judge I want. He understands the real meaning of a contest."

Iizuka was promoted to ninth dan in 1937 and tenth dan in 1948.

Shuichi Nagaoka

Shuichi Nagaoka (1876–1952) was a student of both Kito ryu and Takeuchi ryu jujutsu in his hometown in Okayama Prefecture prior to entering the Kodokan in 1893. With such experience, Nagaoka's rise through the ranks was rapid; he was sixth dan by 1904.

Like all of Kano's disciples, Nagaoka was constantly scolded for bad behavior. At the same time, Kano was always solicitous towards his students. Once, Nagaoka fell very ill with the flu accompanied by a high fever. At the time, Nagaoka was living in the trainees' dormitory. Kano told him, "You will never be able to recover in such a cramped and noisy place, so stay at my house." Kano checked on Nagaoka's condition throughout the night, and made sure that he was covered by enough blankets.

Nagaoka was very skilled in all aspects of judo, especially *sutemi*, "sacrifice throws." Nagaoka reputedly had a match with Shiro Saigo. As mentioned, Saigo continued teaching judo even after his expulsion from the Kodokan. One day in 1897, Saigo is said to have dropped unannounced into the Kodokan, where Nagaoka was training at the time. Upstart Nagaoka requested a match with the legendary Saigo. Saigo agreed but found that he had a hard time throwing Nagaoka even with his trademark yama-arashi technique. Nagaoka could do nothing against Saigo, but at least Nagaoka didn't end up on the mat. Saigo complimented Nagaoka on his potential. (This is another episode that cannot be verified one way or the other.)

Nagaoka (then fourth dan) defeated Demon Yokoyama (then sixth dan) at the kagami-biraki in 1899. The paring of thirty-seven-year-old sixth dan Yokoyama with twenty-three-year-old fourth dan Nagaoka raised some eyebrows. Nagaoka was at the top of his game; Yokoyama was fourteen years older, and as the senior instructor at the Kodokan, he naturally did much more teaching than training for contests. Yokoyama had been known to clash with Kano regarding the nature of contest judo. He maintained that contests should be more martial and realistic but thus more dangerous, something that Kano did not want. It seems that Kano was putting Yokoyama in his place by making him face the younger Nagaoka to prove that judo did work better than an old-style jujutsu approach (although Nagaoka in fact had extensive jujutsu experience himself).

Nagaoka's other memorable match was with Isogai. In 1934, a martial art demonstration was held before the emperor at the Seinenkan Hall on the grounds of the imperial palace. Although it was not originally on the schedule, there was a special request for a match between the two ninth dan masters. Isogai (who was officially retired) was sixty-four at the time; Nagaoka, fifty-nine. Even though it was supposed to be a demonstration match, neither ninth dan wanted to lose or even get thrown as a demonstration. (They had formally competed against each other when they were fifth dan—Nagaoka won. And when they were seventh dan, Isogai prevailed.) The match was an extraordinary display of subtle interaction between the two masters. When it ended in a clear draw, the two were likely much relieved. (Incidentally, both Isogai and Nagaoka had entered the Kodokan when Kano was absent in Kumamoto. Isogai was about a year ahead, but after Nagaoka joined the Kodokan, they spent hours and hours training together.)

Regarding Kano, Nagaoka, and Isogai, Nagaoka wrote that the three of them would often train in no-holds-barred sessions late into the night, researching various techniques. Once, when Isogai tried to escape from a pin applied by Kano, the pin was so secure that Kano broke several of Isogai's ribs.

Since Nagaoka was one of Kano's most trusted disciples, he often accompanied his master as an assistant on Kano's important travels at home and abroad. Nagaoka recalled that on such trips, Kano would suddenly grip Nagaoka's kimono from the front or the back and demand, "Nagaoka! How would you respond if you were attacked like this?" Kano told Nagaoka, "No matter where you are, you are in a dojo."

Nagaoka had a long career teaching in both western and eastern Japan. He was promoted to ninth dan in 1930 and to tenth dan in 1937.

Kyuzo Mifune

Kyuzo Mifune (1883–1965) was the most talented and influential of the second generation of Kodokan instructors, his career spanning the prewar and postwar periods. Mifune was born in Kuji, Iwate Prefecture. He was incorrigible as a child, playing tricks on everyone, stealing fruit from neighboring gardens, and in general causing all kinds of mischief, although he was never a bully. After graduating from elementary school, Mifune got a job at the local city hall. That lasted two weeks. At a loss for what to do with his naughty son, Mifune's father sent him to study in Sendai. Mifune was quite intelligent, but once he discovered judo in middle school, that is what he did the rest of his life.

Mifune went to Tokyo, ostensibly for further study, but actually all he wanted was to enter the Kodokan. In 1903, Mifune got his wish. Mifune showed up at Demon Yokoyama's door to request permission to enter the Kodokan. Yokoyama asked Mifune if he had a letter of introduction. Mifune showed him a copy of *Kokushi*, the journal published by the Kodokan. Yokoyama said, "That's a magazine, not a letter of introduction." Mifune replied, "This journal contains the splendid teachings of Master Kano. I came from Sendai to train under him by all means." Impressed by Mifune's ardor, Yokoyama accepted Mifune as his student at the Kodokan.

Mifune trained relentlessly under Demon Yokoyama. Mifune also enjoyed working out with Maeda, the other demon at the Kodokan. While not quite as small as Saigo, Mifune was not a big man, but that did not stop him: "I am grateful to my parents for giving me a small body. In order to overcome bigger opponents, I have to train twice as hard."

Mifune's motto was, "If my opponents train one hour, I will train two. If they train two, I will train three." As a young man, Mifune was another one who liked to test his judo skills on the street. He reportedly had to be bailed out by Kano more than a few times. There is a touching story about Kano in Mifune's memoirs:

> Since I was always misbehaving in my younger days, I got nothing but scolding from Master Kano. On a teaching trip to Hokkaido, I developed an acute viral infection and went into septic shock. It was touch and go at the hospital. A telegram arrived from Master Kano: "Mifune, don't get thrown!" That simple message of support brought tears to my eyes, and raised my spirit immensely. I recovered.

He also observed:

> Even though a number of us had nicknames such as "Demon," "Destroyer," or "Killer," all of the senior students looked up to Master Kano with the highest regard. Sakujiro Yokoyama, who would not stand down for anyone else, always bowed deeply in respect whenever he greeted Master Kano.

Over the years, Mifune's technique became nearly flawless, considered by many be second only to Saigo. It is believed that Mifune was never defeated in formal competition—he even threw a fellow seventh dan in one memorable demonstration match. Although well versed in every judo technique, Mifune's trademark was kuki-nage, "air throw." Kuki-nage is a kind of corner throw, which Mifune executed seamlessly, with perfect timing and control.

By age thirty, Mifune was sixth dan. In 1937, the year before his death, Kano promoted Mifune to ninth dan. After Kano passed away, Mifune became the principal instructor of the Kodokan and was largely responsible for the expansion of judo in the postwar period at home and abroad. His technique was incomparable. In 1956, Mifune published the *Canon of Judo*, an extensive training manual. His amazing ability can be seen in a film in which the seventy-three-year-old Mifune demonstrates judo against a series of young Japanese and foreign trainees. (The film is available on DVD with the English title *The Essence of Judo—Kyuzo Mifune, the God of Judo*.)

Like Kano, Mifune was a judo philosopher. Here are two of Mifune's teachings:

The Five Principal Points of Judo

1. The soft controls the hard.
2. Strike to kill (resolve any problem with a single decisive action).
3. Do not hold anything back (never be tentative).
4. Enter a state of no-self, no-mind.
5. Do not place hope in finding a secret technique. Polish the mind through ceaseless training; that is the key to effective techniques.

Seven Rules of Judo Practice

1. Do not make light of any opponent.
2. Do not lose self-confidence.
3. Maintain good posture.
4. Develop speed.
5. Project power in all directions.
6. Never stop training.
7. Develop self-control.

Mifune actually composed a judo song that was put to music and meant to be sung out loud:

When you train, free yourself from distracting thoughts;
Keep your heart buoyant, your body buoyant too.
Do not forget the principle of "return to the center";
Strive and strive, with single-minded devotion.
This is our judo!
This is our judo!

Accumulate skill through ceaseless forging of body and mind;

Attain the miraculous power of seven times down, eight
    times up.
Awaken to the path of liberation;
Become like a rotating ball, effortlessly responding to any
    contingency.
This is our judo!
This is our judo!

The path of softness transcends national borders:
A pliant heart has no enemies,
People of the world join hands,
And establish an ideal global village.
This is our judo!
This is our judo!

Mifune had a good sense of judo humor. Once, he visited a karate dojo where, in a demonstration, the instructor broke a stack of tiles with a single blow of his thickly callused fist. He challenged Mifune: "Can a judo man do this?" Mifune replied, "Yes, very easily." "Show me." Mifune said, "OK, set up the tiles." While the tiles were being set up, Mifune fetched a hammer from his bag. (He had been expecting such a challenge.) "You are going to use that to smash the tiles?" "Of course," said Mifune. "In judo, this is what we call 'efficient use of energy.' What it took you years of practice to accomplish, we can do in a second," Mifune said as he smashed the pile to smithereens with the hammer.

Mifune could be sneaky as well. At the 1930 kagami-biraki, Mifune was scheduled to have a master's demonstration with Tsunetane Ota. Mifune was Ota's senior, but, as mentioned, Ota was very skilled at groundwork, so he would try to fight the match on the mat. For the first time, the kagami-biraki was going to be held in public at an exhibition hall in Hibiya Park. The evening before, Mifune visited Ota. He told Ota, "Let's put on a good demonstration match tomorrow." He gave Ota a gift of money: "Treat yourself to a drink." Ota was a heavy drinker, so Mifune knew Ota would get smashed. For his part, Ota thought, "Yes, let's put on a good show. I will keep standing during the match and take a breakfall or two for my senior Mifune."

During the demonstration match, Mifune unexpectedly lowered the boom on Ota, throwing him nearly twenty feet. The cameramen present caught Mifune's throw of Ota. The following day's newspaper carried a large photo of the scene with the caption "Master Mifune Throws Ota Like a Leaf." Ota never forgave Mifune.

Mifune was promoted to tenth dan in 1945. During the sixty-two-year period from his entrance into the Kodokan in 1903 to 1964, the year before his death, Mifune never missed a day of official training. Mifune died of throat cancer in 1965.

Sambo Toku

Sambo Toku (1887–1945) was the all-time Kodokan fighting champion in Japan, even more so than his hero Saigo. From early on, Toku, who was born in Kagoshima, was actually nicknamed "Saigo." In elementary school, he started striking trees with a wooden sword a thousand times a night. Once, there was a fire at Toku's elementary school dormitory, and Toku was trapped on the second floor. He leaped out of a window imagining he was delivering a flying sword cut to a nearby pine tree. It worked: he landed safely. After that, like Saigo, Toku started jumping from tall places in order to practice landing squarely on his feet. However, unlike Saigo, Toku was large, powerful, and menacing looking, even as a kid.

When he was a child, Toku had fights with every other kid in his neighborhood. In middle school, he was thrown out of the kendo club for trying to cut the instructor in half with a sword (although the instructor had asked for it, daring any student in the club to hit him with a live blade; the instructor only wore a chest protector, which Toku nearly sawed in two with his sword cut).

In high school, he was engaged in two epic battles involving dozens of people, most of whom the teenage Toku thrashed. One was in the fish market. A stall keeper spilled wastewater on Toku when he passed by. A fight ensued, first between Toku and the stall keeper, and then with the nearby stall keepers who rushed to the first one's aid. (Toku was beating him unmercifully.) The second occurred on a bridge. A bunch of porters made fun of Toku dressed in his school uniform (which was too small for him). Again, the hot-tempered youth challenged them collectively to a fight, resulting in a melee and many injuries to the porters. Toku was arrested and consequently expelled from school.

In light of such fierce behavior, it is no wonder Toku quickly established himself as the top judo competitor in Kagoshima. He had started judo in middle school. His first teacher was Kaishiro Samura (1880–1964, later tenth dan). Toku would not give up during training with Samura even if he got knocked out. As soon as he revived, Toku would plead, "One more match. One more match." The training sessions did not stop until Samura said, "That's enough for today." Toku won every competition he entered, demolishing each opponent. Samura recommended Toku for admittance to the Kano Academy and the Kodokan. Kano accepted Toku but told him, "You must finish middle school. You can do that when you are in Tokyo." Toku was admitted to the Kodokan in May 1906.

Toku had such a dark, swarthy complexion that most people mistook him for an Okinawan, Chinese, or some other kind of exotic Asian. His hair was short and bristly, his eyes sharp and intense. Big, broad-shouldered, and with arms as thick as his legs, Toku stood out immediately at the Kodokan. He threw himself into training, trying to engage in at least one hundred contests a day. He was always the first at the dojo—in those days, practice began at 5:00 A.M.—even though he lived five miles away and had to walk because no trains ran at that hour. Even when he overdid it and broke his arm, he continued to train full-time with his arm in a wooden splint. Toku refused to take practice breakfalls because "I don't need to—no one will be able to throw me." Indeed, Toku's nickname was "The Pine Tree in the Middle of the Field" because his legs seemed rooted to the earth. Toku was third dan in a little more than a year.

Kyuzo Mifune (*left*) and Sambo Toku (*right*).

Toku was, in fact, nearly impossible to throw, even for the likes of Kyuzo Mifune. Mifune and Toku, fifth dan and third dan, respectively, at the time, had a spectacular match at the kaga-mi-biraki in January 1910. Although Toku was much bigger and stronger than Mifune, the master technician Mifune controlled the match, even when Toku became enraged as he was wont to do. Mifune had Toku in a choke hold at the end, but Toku refused to submit. Yamashita, who was the judge, called a halt to the match. However, because of Toku's performance against the best judo man in the world, Toku was awarded fourth dan on the spot. Kodokan judo men have always had trouble with matches against groundwork experts. Actually, it was Kodokan men in Tokyo who had trouble with groundwork experts because Kano disliked groundwork, and discouraged its application in judo contests as detrimental to the flow of action. Standing techniques were much to be preferred. It was in the outlying districts where groundwork judo was the mainstay. In March 1910, an expert in groundwork from Okayama named Kotaro Okano came to the Kodokan for a seminar. He easily defeated the first five high-ranking Tokyo judo men he faced by getting them on the ground and pinning or choking them out, leaving only Mifune to face him. Demon Yokoyama ran to get Demon Toku to avoid the possibility of Mifune losing to Okano. Toku was not present because he was laid up with a high fever. After dousing himself with cold water, Toku came to the rescue of the Tokyo Kodokan standing technique. Toku avoided the groundwork issue altogether by throwing Okano off the mat before he could attempt anything. Okano was knocked out.

In May of the same year, Toku had the match of matches with Shotaro Tabata. The competition was in a similar vein, Kanto Kodokan judo versus Kansai Kodokan judo. It was Champion of the East Toku versus Champion of the West Tabata. Isogai (head instructor of Osaka judo and an expert in groundwork) was the referee. Shortly after the match began, Tabata executed a throw on Toku. Toku left the ground only a few inches, and it was not a clean throw by any means, more like a half. To everyone's surprise, Isogai called it a clean fall in favor of Tabata, perhaps on the peculiar grounds that since Tabata had gotten Toku in the air, that was enough. There was no appealing the decision, but there was a second round, which Toku won with a pin. Thus, a third round was required. In this final round, Toku and Tabata were trying to kill each other, so Isogai called out, "That's enough!" The two still continued to struggle, so Isogai had to break them apart. Although there was still time left on the clock, Isogai declared, "The match is over. It is a draw."

Alas, Kano had his hands full trying to rein in Toku. Kano had a soft spot for the rascal Toku, but his reckless behavior in the street—Toku would immediately run to participate in any kind of "boxer or wrestler against all comers" sideshow that he heard about—and rough treatment of trainees in the dojo was damaging the Kodokan's reputation. In 1912, a group of Brazilian sailors, who had some experience of jujutsu learned from a Japanese immigrant in their home country, petitioned the Kodokan for challenge matches. Toku demolished them all, injuring four or five of them seriously through excessive use of force. The event became an international incident when the Brazilian embassy lodged a formal complaint with the Japanese government. Although Kano was abroad at the time the incident occurred, he had no choice but to expel Toku from the Kodokan. Like Saigo, Toku had been expelled from the Kodokan for fighting when Kano was overseas. Toku was twenty-five years old.

Toku also lost his job as a judo instructor at the middle school where he was teaching. Ever considerate, Kano sent Toku an envelope with money to assist him until he got on his feet again. Toku was grateful but he couldn't accept it, despite the fact that he was penniless.

Toku hit the road, attempting to teach at various dojos along the way. Because he was no longer an official Kodokan instructor, he could not get paid, nor stay for more than a few days. It is said that he was defeated by Senya Kunii (1894–1966), head master of the Kashima Shin ryu, in a challenge match and became Kunii's student for a time.

In any event, Toku ended up back in Kagoshima, where he enlisted in the military as a member of a gunnery squad. Although it is hard to believe, Toku got into a fight with an ornery stallion used to pull the cannons. The horse kicked Toku in the side, breaking two of his ribs. Toku replied with a punch to the horse's mouth that knocked the animal out. Toku's injury was so serious he was hospitalized for two months and then discharged from the military for reasons of health.

Toku went to Kyoto to try to get a job at the Martial Art Academy there, but Isogai and the other Kodokan instructors turned him down because of his expulsion. Toku then went to Shikoku.

There are always hundreds of pilgrims there on the eighty-eight-temple circuit. Since the local people are very kind, providing food for pilgrims—even those who are vagrants, not pilgrims—it is possible to survive. Toku began training by himself in the mountains, running up and down temple steps, lifting heavy boulders, and striking thick trees with his fists. One day, walking along a mountain path, he encountered a *yamabushi* (one of the wizard priests who hide out in the mountains). Many yamabushi in those days were actually rogue martial artists expelled from their dojos for bad behavior (like Toku) or renegades wanted by the police. Some of them were highwaymen in disguise. The powerful-looking yamabushi called himself Tenshobo. When he learned Toku was a judo man, he sneered. "Fighting in a dojo on mats is for sissies. The real test of your skill is fighting outdoors in the open!" An altercation between the two ensued. Toku got knocked out. He woke up in the hut of a woodcutter being fed rice gruel. A little later, Toku ran across a group of wild young men practicing punches, high kicks, and leaps from cliff to cliff, and also practicing using a priest's staff as a weapon. They let Toku join in the training. The group never stayed in one place for long. They were like gypsies, setting up camp deep in the mountains here and there, and subsisting on fruit, nuts, wild mushrooms, soba flour, honey from beehives, and sometimes snakes. After a few years of training like this, Toku became good enough to hold his own against Tenshobo.

More important, during his time in the mountains, Toku did a lot of soul-searching about the real purpose of judo and the meaning of Kano's teachings. In 1917, Toku got back to Tokyo and asked to be readmitted to the Kodokan. Kano said, "I've been expecting you. I'll consider letting you back in, but first I need to see your judo." Kano had Toku square off against Toda, a rising young star of the Kodokan. Toku's judo was much more composed and refined than before. Kano said, "You've learned something. Welcome back."

Toku needed to show his stuff to the Kodokan public. Kano refereed a match between Toku and Shunzo Ishida, another young star. Kano declared the match a draw. However, at the end, Ishida could barely walk, and Toku had not broken a sweat. Toku wanted to demonstrate his newfound self-control and lack of a need to destroy his opponent.

In the following years, Toku was a proper Kodokan instructor rather than a madman. Toku taught at Waseda and other universities. In 1930, at the age of forty-five, Toku was defeated for the first time in a public match, by sixth dan Ryou Uto. Kano had asked Toku to participate, and Toku agreed despite the fact that he'd recently had pneumonia. The rumor spread: "Toku's losing it." However, the next year in another public demonstration, the fully recovered Toku threw seven opponents in a row, their ranks ranging from third to sixth dan. "Toku still has it" was the updated rumor.

Toku died during the Tokyo air raid on March 10, 1945. It is said that he and his wife drowned in the Sumida River while trying to save the children who had jumped into the water to avoid the flames. Toku was promoted to eighth dan in 1937 and ninth dan posthumously upon his death in 1945. Together with Saigo and Mifune, Toku is one of the great Kodokan legends.

Masaya Suzuki

Many of Kano's trainees at the Kodokan became important industrialists. Masaya Suzuki (1861–1922) was the third director general of the Sumitomo Conglomerate. Suzuki was also a student of Tesshu Yamaoka. Suzuki was a keen Zen student all his life, both in the meditation hall and in the workplace. He joked, "I have many more difficult koan to solve in business than I ever had in the Zendo." As leader of one of the largest commercial concerns in the country, Suzuki made Zen Buddhism, combined with Kano's *jita kyoei* ("mutual well-being") philosophy, his business model. Throughout his tenure as director general, Suzuki endeavored to make all Sumitomo's enterprises a benefit to the nation and its citizens. Since Suzuki believed that "workers make the enterprise," he established many benefits for Sumitomo workers—health care, housing, pensions, and other support. (Remember, this was at the beginning of the twentieth century.) Suzuki also directed the extensive reforestation of areas damaged by Sumitomo mining. Enlightened.

Keita Goto

Keita Goto (1882–1959) was born to a family of farmers in the remote mountain village of Aoki in Nagano Prefecture. Goto did not receive a Confucian samurai education like Kano but was raised in a pious rural atmosphere. His father made the Nichiren chant, "Namu Ho Myo Rengekyo," from five hundred to one thousand times a day.

Although money was very tight, Goto managed to make it through high school. After working as a middle school teacher in his hometown for a few years to raise money, in 1902 Goto went to Tokyo to take the entrance exam to the Tokyo School of Commerce. Goto flunked the English section of the exam. Next summer Goto tried Kano's Tokyo Teacher Training College and made it in successfully. As a challenge, Goto entered the department of English literature.

In 1906, he graduated from Tokyo Teacher Training College. In 1907, Goto, who desired the best education possible regardless of the obstacles, passed the entrance exam to Tokyo University, this time enrolling in the law department. Kano, Goto's favorite teacher at Tokyo Teacher Training College, helped Goto financially during this period by arranging for Goto to become the live-in tutor at the home of the wealthy Baron Fujii. Goto never forgot Kano's support, and considered Kano to have been one of the main influences in his life.

After graduation from Tokyo University in 1911, Goto entered the Agricultural Ministry and then the Transportation Ministry. Goto retired from the ministry in 1920 to become director of a small railway company. In the ensuing years, by shrewd and aggressive acquisition, development projects, and prudent investing (along with government clout), Goto built a huge railroad, real estate, department store, hotel, and educational facility empire, the Tokyu Group. Goto, nicknamed the "Japanese Robber Baron," was one of the richest businessmen in Japan, if not the richest. In 1944, Goto served as transport and communication minister in the Tojo cabinet. Even though Goto was banned from conducting any business activity by the GHQ in 1947, Goto remained a force behind the scenes, and actively resumed his business career by 1950. Following the war, Goto became much less cutthroat and more generous with donations to many charitable causes. Goto's son recalled that "for the last ten years of his life, my father did nothing but lose money."

Goto was a keen patron of the arts as well as a skilled amateur potter himself. In 1960, the Gotoh Museum was established in Tokyo to house his magnificent collection of Japanese and Asian art, likely the best such collection in private hands.

Matsutaro Shoriki

Matsutaro Shoriki (1885–1969) may have not been quite as wealthy as Goto, but he was a more influential and important social figure. Shoriki was an entrepreneur extraordinaire, media mogul, business tycoon, sportsman, politician, and philanthropist. Shoriki, born in Toyama, started judo in middle school. In 1907, he entered Tokyo University and the Kodokan. Shoriki practiced judo more than he studied but managed to both graduate and attain third dan in 1911. Shoriki was a student of Demon Yokoyama. Once, he went to visit Yokoyama when his teacher was on his deathbed. As he approached Yokoyama's house, the dogs in the neighborhood started barking madly. As in many cultures, dogs barking like that are thought to be a sign of a soul's passing. Concerned, Shoriki went into the house. Yokoyama was in bed but still alive, and said with a smile, "It will take more than a few barking dogs to finish me off."

Shoriki started working for the metropolitan police in 1913, serving until 1924. Thereafter, he founded the *Yomiuri* newspaper; the Japanese Professional Baseball League (with the Yomiuri Giants as the top team); and Japan's first commercial television station, Nippon Television Network Corporation; and served as the first chairman of Japan's Atomic Energy Commission. He survived a right-wing assassination attempt in 1934—the fanatic was furious that Shoriki had allowed an American baseball team to play in sacred Jingu stadium—but was left with a sixteen-inch-long scar on his back. He was appointed to the House of Peers in 1944 and elected to the House of Representatives in 1955. Shoriki served as the minister of the Hokkaido Development Agency and then the Japanese Science and Technology Agency. Among many other charitable activities was the endowment of the chair of the Department of Asia, Oceania, and Africa at the Museum of Fine Arts in Boston.

On the downside, as a police chief, Shoriki was accused by the Korean government of inciting the massacre of ethnic Koreans by spreading rumors of people of that nationality looting and killing Japanese in the chaos following the 1923 Great Kanto Earthquake. After the war, Shoriki was imprisoned as a class A war criminal but was released in 1947. Recently discovered documents stored in the National Archives and Records Administration in Washington, D.C., indicate that Shoriki was a CIA agent, given support to establish a media friendly to the United States and promote a nuclear energy program—with American technology—in Japan. (Understandably, most Japanese wanted nothing to do with nuclear power.)

Shoriki did not have much time to train in judo after his promotion to fifth dan in 1926, but he remained the Kodokan's main promoter. He was the financial force behind the construction of the new Kodokan headquarters in 1958. Not surprisingly, given the extent of his massive financial support, Shoriki was awarded tenth dan upon his death in 1969, the first "nonprofessional" to be accorded that honor.

Shiso Kanakuri

One non-judo disciple of Kano was the marathon runner Shiso Kanakuri (1891–1984). Kanakuri was a physical education major at the Tokyo Teacher Training College. In the qualifying trials for the 1912 Stockholm Olympics, Kanakuri broke the world record for the marathon, at that time a distance of twenty-five miles. Kanakuri's time was 2 hours, 32 minutes, and 45 seconds. Naturally, Kanakuri was selected to represent Japan at the Olympics—and Kano, as president of the College and member of the Olympic Committee, of course supported the decision. However, Kanakuri lacked the confidence to perform on an international stage and visited Kano's office to ask his permission to withdraw. Kano gave him the "It is not about winning, it is about how you play the game" pep talk and refused to accept Kanakuri's withdrawal.

Kanakuri's participation in the 1912 Stockholm Olympics is legendary. After a demanding twenty-day trip by ship and the Trans-Siberian Railway, Kanakuri arrived in Stockholm. He could not stomach the food and could not sleep because there was almost no night during that season in Sweden. The vehicle that was supposed to pick Kanakuri up on race day never showed so he had to run to the stadium. At race time, the temperature was a sweltering 104 degrees Fahrenheit. Out of sixty-eight runners, half dropped out, and one of them died the day after the race. After Kanakuri got about halfway, he stopped at a farmhouse (the route ran through the country) to get a drink of water. Suffering badly from sunstroke, Kanakuri fell asleep on the couch and did not wake up until the next morning. The officials listed Kanakuri as "missing enroute, whereabouts unknown." Kanakuri finally turned up acutely embarrassed. Kanakuri was so ashamed that he did not want to return to Japan. Kano, though, was forgiving and in fact sponsored Kanakuri's future participation in the 1920 Antwerp Olympics (he placed sixteenth) and the 1924 Paris Olympics (he dropped out.) Unfortunately, Kanakuri's best chance for a medal would have been the 1916 Olympics in Berlin, but the event was cancelled because of World War I. In 1967, at the invitation of the Stockholm Olympic Commemoration Committee, Kanakuri returned to the stadium. A goal was set up, and after completing a trot around the track, Kanakuri crossed the finish line. His time, a world record likely never to be surpassed: 54 years, 8 months, 6 days, 32 minutes 3 seconds. Afterwards, Kanakuri joked, "It was long race. I had five grandchildren before it was over."

Kanakuri considered Kano a second father and sought Kano's counsel over the years. Kano arranged for him to coach at the Teacher Training College, and later Kanakuri went on to become the "Father of Marathon Running in Japan."

Shinzo Takagaki

Shinzo Takagaki (1893–1977), mentioned earlier in relation to Rabindranath Tagore, was the "Father of Judo in Asia" as well as an important judo missionary to South America. Takagaki began his practice of jujutsu when he was twelve years old, and then entered the Kodokan at age sixteen. Takagaki was fourth dan by the time he was a college student. After graduation from Nihon University, Takagaki went to Canada to study at the University of British Columbia in Vancouver and established the judo dojo there. During his stay on the Pacific Coast, the local Japanese community organized a "Friendship Match" for Takagaki, hoping to show the white folk the superiority of Japanese judo. The 140-pound Takagaki was pitted against the 240-pound champion wrestler Dick Daviscot in a no-holds-barred challenge match held in Tacoma, Washington. The match went on for an hour and twenty minutes. Not surprisingly, the Japanese account has Takagaki in the lead, with a firm choke hold on Daviscot when the bell saved the American wrestler. Although the match was declared a draw, once again the Japanese claimed a moral victory because of the difference in size between the two competitors.

After three years in Canada, Takagaki returned to Japan. As mentioned, Takagaki was recruited to go to India (reportedly at the recommendation of Mitsuru Toyama). Takagaki demonstrated judo all over India; Indira Gandhi, seven years old at the time, was said to have attended one of the demonstrations. After two years of teaching judo in India, Takagaki went to Nepal at the request of its king. Takagaki defeated a large local wrestler in front of the king, greatly impressing His Majesty.

Over the ensuing years, Takagaki taught judo in Afghanistan, Burma, Thailand, Malaysia, Java, Sumatra, and Taiwan. It is quite likely that besides teaching judo in those countries, Takagaki was gathering valuable intelligence—in other words, he was a spy. However, this was par for the course for many Japanese working in Asia at the time, and it was pretty much accepted by the Japanese that this is what one did when traveling abroad. (When Yamashita was in the United States, he was the perfect person to gather intelligence on the country's political, industrial, and military capabilities due to his access to the highest levels of American leadership, including the president.)

In 1952, at the invitation of Juan Perón, Takagaki taught in Argentina, and then in Brazil, Peru, Mexico, Cuba, and the United States—not as a spy this time, for the war was over.

In his later years in Japan, Takagaki became a respected teacher to both Japanese and foreign students. Takagaki's judo was said to be flexible, almost delicate; he could throw opponents with the softest movements without their realizing what was happening. He said ground techniques should be executed like "an infant turning over in its sleep."

When Takagaki developed kidney stones, he went to the beach to do breakfall after breakfall to, as he said, "shake the stones loose."

Takagaki's book, coauthored with Harold E. Sharp, *The Techniques of Judo*, is still in print.

Keishichi Ishiguro

Keishichi Ishiguro (1897–1974) was another judo missionary, in this case to Europe and the Middle East. In addition to being a judo instructor, Ishiguro was a radio comedian and a collector. He was born in Niigata Prefecture and started judo in middle school. As a student at Waseda University, Ishiguro entered the Kodokan in 1915. He rose quickly through the ranks and was fifth dan by 1924. At age twenty-seven, Ishiguro on his own established a "Send Ishiguro to France" supporters group. The money was somehow raised, and off he went to Paris to teach judo.

Improbably, Ishiguro hooked up with the eccentric and flamboyant Tsuguharu Fujita (1886–1968), a well-known and successful Parisian artist. He was a cross-dresser, decking himself out in the most outlandish costumes—wearing, for example, a Greek tunic or a floral curtain wrapped about him and sporting huge gold earrings. Fujita is the last person you would think of as a martial artist, but actually he came from a samurai family. He had trained diligently in judo at the middle school where Kano was principal. Fujita was second dan. To introduce Ishiguro and Kodokan judo to the public, the two staged a demonstration at the Paris Opera House. Fujita, dressed in a somber judogi rather than one of his gaudy outfits, attacked Ishiguro with a sword. Ishiguro countered with an impressive display of judo disarming techniques. Fujita then threw Ishiguro. Fujita got carried away, and Ishiguro landed offstage. Ishiguro was injured, and had to use crutches for a while after the demonstration was finished. The demonstration was a big hit, giving Ishiguro's career as a judo teacher in Europe an important boost.

After a successful stay spreading judo in Europe and giving classes in Egypt, Ishiguro returned to Japan in 1933. Following the war, Ishiguro worked as an essayist, and then for some years was a regular cast member on the popular radio comedy program *Tonchi Kyoshitsu*. Ishiguro also amassed a huge collection of arts and crafts, photos of which have been published in many volumes. He was judo seventh dan.

Sumiyuki Kotani

Although Sumiyuki Kotani (1903–91) was one of the men who participated as a member of the unsuccessful Japanese wrestling team in the 1932 Olympics, he was always primarily a Kodokan judo man. As a young trainee, Kotani was known as "Reverse Demon." That is, he was a demon for self-punishment. Right from the beginning of his Kodokan training, Kotani sought out the toughest and most powerful judo fighters without regard for his personal well-being. He was thrown, pinned, and strangled in every possible way—for Kotani, the harder, the better. He felt such grueling punishment would make him the strongest fighter he could be.

Kotani can be considered Kano's last direct disciple. Kano

trusted Kotani, and in fact said, "Kotani's judo is the kind I like."
Kano often chose Kotani as a traveling instructor on his teaching
tours overseas. Kotani headed up the International Division of
the Kodokan for many years and is thus responsible for the development of numerous non-Japanese judo instructors. He was
promoted to tenth dan in 1984.

Kenji Tomiki

Kenji Tomiki (1900–1979) was a student of both judo (under
Kano) and aikido (under Ueshiba). Tomiki was born in Akita to
a well-off family and started practicing judo at an early age. Tomiki was both academically and physically gifted in school—he
was an honor student as well as captain of the judo team. Even
though he was robust, Tomiki contracted tuberculosis and was
consequently bedridden for more than three years. Luckily, Tomiki recovered fully and proceeded to enter Waseda University in
Tokyo in 1924. He trained at both the Waseda Judo Club and the
Kodokan. By the end of his senior year, Tomiki was fourth dan.

While still at college, Tomiki was introduced to the martial
art wizard Morihei Ueshiba. Seemingly without effort, Ueshiba
tossed the powerful Tomiki around like a rag doll, and pinned
him with a single finger. Tomiki never stopped his judo practice,
but he also trained intently under Ueshiba, becoming perhaps the
keenest student of Ueshiba's physical techniques. Throughout
the rest of his career, Tomiki attempted to reconcile the rational,
scientific approach of Kano's Kodokan judo (judo close at hand)
with the internal aspects of Ueshiba's aikido (judo at a distance).
Tomiki was a professor, primarily a judo man, who had no interest in Ueshiba's mystical philosophy or his "divinely inspired"
techniques. By dismissing such aspects of Ueshiba's aikido,
though, Tomiki ignored the fact that Ueshiba firmly believed that
his enlightenment made him the master that he was, not any kind
of rational system of exercises and precise body movements.

Tomiki, however, preferred to focus precisely on those elements. He viewed judo as essentially a system of self-defense
rather than mere physical education. Tomiki's *Kodokan Self-De-*

fense Techniques is the textbook for that approach. Tomiki traveled to Manchuria in 1936 to teach budo, and in 1938 assumed a position as martial art instructor at the newly established Kenkoku University, where he taught until 1945. Following his capture by the Soviet Army, he was sent to Siberia, and not repatriated until three years later. Tomiki survived that punishing ordeal, forced to practice judo and aikido movements more in his mind than in his body.

Tomiki returned to a completely different Japan in 1948. What occurred next generated great controversy. Even though it was totally contrary to Ueshiba's fundamental principle that there be no competitive matches in the aikido dojo—aikido was the way of harmony, beyond winning or losing—Tomiki insisted that aikido have a competitive element. Tomiki claimed that aikido needed formal contests to foster "a fighting spirit and practical skills in self-defense." Tomiki devised peculiar rules for official contests. These rules and restrictions satisfied no one except Tomiki and his closest disciples. Tomiki-style aikido never gained more than a very small following.

Nonetheless, Tomiki was never expelled from the official aikido organization, and in fact served as its head. Tomiki devoted his life to judo and aikido, as he interpreted the two systems. Tomiki was awarded eighth dan in both disciplines.

Minoru Mochizuki

Minoru Mochizuki (1907–2003) was another Kodokan judo man who studied with Ueshiba. Actually, Mochizuki was always a mixed martial artist, who practiced just about every martial art available while he was at the Kodokan, encouraged to do so by Kano as a member of the Kodokan Kobujutsu Research Group. Mochizuki's initial judo teacher was Sambo Toku. Mochizuki first encountered Toku when he showed up at the kendo dojo where Mochizuki was practicing. Without any introduction, Toku asked to borrow a set of kendo gear and join the practice matches. Mochizuki thought he would teach this impertinent upstart a good lesson, and lent him gear. When the match began,

Mochizuki swept down with his feared "demon killer cut." The instant before his bamboo sword would have landed on the side of Toku's head, Mochizuki felt as if a pair of hot tongs had pierced his throat. Toku had countered with a thrust. Mochizuki said that the reason his voice always sounded hoarse was as a result of Toku's thrust damaging his vocal cords. Toku later told Mochizuki that he came to the dojo to see how good his own kendo was. In Kagoshima, he'd never had anyone of high level to train with in kendo, so he turned to judo. However, he still liked kendo and wanted to see how he would test against top-rated opponents. Toku did pretty well. Thereafter, Mochizuki entered Toku's judo dojo.

When Mochizuki was a student, he lived with his sister in Tsurumi. Since the house was more than twenty miles from the Kodokan, Mochizuki had to leave at midnight to make it for the 4:00 A.M. starting time of training during kan-geiko. He had to walk because there were no trains in the middle of the night. When Mifune saw Mochizuki one frigid morning breaking the ice in the well near the Kodokan to get a drink, he asked him, "Where did you come from?" When Mochizuki told him, "Tsurumi," Mifune exclaimed, "You idiot! You will die of exhaustion if you keep that up for thirty days. Stay at my place." Thus, Mochizuki became a live-in disciple of Mifune.

When Mochizuki proudly reported to Kano, "Today I won two tournaments, held at different colleges," Kano replied, "So that is why you are training in judo? To win tournaments? You should have first told me what you learned today from your experiences, not whether or not you won!"

Mochizuki went on to attain high ranks in judo, aikido, jujutsu, kendo, *iaido*, *kobudo*, karate, *jojutsu*, and so forth, although of some these ranks were obtained from groups under his auspices. He signed himself "Minoru Mochizuki, the master with sixty dans." He founded the Yoseikan dojo in Shizuoka, and formed the Kokusai Budoin, an international martial arts organization to promote his unique style of teaching.

Yasushi Inoue

Yasushi Inoue (1907–91) is one of twentieth-century Japan's most important literary figures and one of the period's finest writers. His works *Tan-huang, The Blue Wolf: A Novel of the Life of Chinggis Khan, The Samurai Banner of Furin Kazan, Roof Tile of Tempyo,* and several others have been published in English translation. Inoue was a keen judo player (sixth dan) throughout his life, and a devoted student of Jigoro Kano and his teachings. Inoue's novel *North Sea*—unfortunately not available in English translation—is based on his experiences as captain of the judo club at Kanazawa Higher School.

Yukio Tani and Gunji Koizumi

Yukio Tani (1881–1950) and Gunji Koizumi (1885–1965) were converts to Kodokan judo. Koizumi studied a variety of martial arts in Japan before he finally settled in London. Koizumi, with Tani acting as a full-time instructor, opened the Budokwai in 1918, mainly teaching jujutsu. Kano visited the Budokwai in 1920 and persuaded both men to agree to join the Kodokan and accept judo second dan. Koizumi was an instructor after Kano's heart—founder of several charitable societies as well as sponsor of a dojo. Koizumi was a scholar and expert on Japanese lacquerware. In addition to cataloging the Victoria and Albert Museum's collection of lacquerware, Koizumi published the definitive study on the subject. Tani, in contrast, was exactly the kind of professional jujutsu fighter that Kano deplored. Most of the years Tani had been in London, he was a successful music hall entertainer-brawler, taking on all comers. Nevertheless, Kano was very keen for both of them to join the Kodokan, even though he knew that they would never actually be changing their teaching style to orthodox Kodokan judo. Kano really wanted to turn the Budokwai into the London branch of the Kodokan, but that did not happen. However, Koizumi did go on to help found the British Judo Association and the European Judo Federation.

Tatsukuma Ushijima

An appalling example of how far judo contests had degenerated from Kano's ideal is the reprimand Tatsukuma (Dragon Bear) Ushijima (1904–85) gave to his student Masahiko Kimura (1917–93). In a contest, Kimura had defeated eight fourth dan opponents in a row. Exhausted, Kimura lost the ninth match. Rather than complimenting Kimura on his accomplishment—Kimura was immediately promoted to fifth dan because of his performance—Ushijima slapped him, and berated Kimura with these words: "A contest is like a fight to the death. To defeat an opponent in a match is equivalent to killing him. Being defeated means to be killed. You killed eight enemies in the contest, but got killed by the ninth. You can only survive in judo by killing or drawing with your opponent, no matter how many you face. To lose is to die."

Ushijima was as extreme a competitor and coach as Hatta. Ushijima was born in Kumamoto, where there was more jujutsu than judo. The jujutsu style was extreme—there was no such thing as a draw. The match went on until one of the competitors gave up or died. Some matches were fought with a wooden dagger kept in one's belt. If you pinned your opponent, you could mimic cutting off his head with the dagger. Ushijima's judo was the same: "Attack, attack, attack." Ushijima visited every dojo he could find to engage anyone who was willing in randori and spent much of his nights lifting heavy boulders and striking trees with his hands to build his strength. The night before a match, he drank turtle's blood. On the morning of the match, he ate powder made from the body of a poison adder. He would seclude himself in a cave for a week doing Zazen and reading *Musashi's Book of Five Rings*. Ushijima was all-Japan champion in 1931 and 1932. He nearly trained himself to death, developing a life-threatening viral infection that ended his career. Ushijima retired from competition in 1934, thereafter devoting himself to making Kimura the world's top fighter. In 1951 in Brazil, Kimura defeated Helio Grace in one of the most famous matches in martial arts history. Kano was long gone by then.

Muneo Shiotani

Muneo Shiotani (1906–85) had the highest regard for Kano the man—Shiotani did the survey of Kano's calligraphy mentioned in chapter 5 and served as a member of the Judo Medical Research Group—but he was dissatisfied with the niceties of Kodokan judo. After he left the Kodokan, Shiotani went on to develop Sogobujutsu Kakutojutsu (Grand System of All the Fighting Arts). As the name implies, it was a mixed martial arts system with everything in it but the kitchen sink, based on actual combat situations, including fighting outdoors in the fields and mountains. The group's last public demonstration was interrupted by the bombs falling on Osaka during a World War II air raid. Nonetheless, the demonstrators continued on to the end, evidently confident that they could dodge the bombs. After the war, Shiotani created a new system he called *Maboroshi no Butsu*, "Phantom Bujutsu." Shiotani now contended that the practice of his system would make war a phantom, never again to plague humankind. No more war was always the purpose of Kodokan judo.

Kano's Female Students

Kano often said, "If you really want to understand judo, watch the women train." The first judo student, male or female, was Kano's oldest sister, Katsuko. When Kano came home after jujutsu training, he taught her some of the moves he had learned that day at the dojo. Here are the stories of a few of Kano's outstanding female students.

Sueko Ashiya and Noriko Yasuda

Kano's first recorded female student was Sueko Ashiya, who approached Tomita with a request to train in judo in 1883. Tomita consulted with Kano, and they agreed to let Ashiya begin judo training. After that, gradually a few women started training in the Gobancho dojo. In 1884, thirty-three-year-old Noriko Yasuda requested permission to practice judo. Yasuda had had a difficult life and was weak and sickly, mentally as well as physically. Kano was confident judo could help her.

Kano made sure Yasuda ate well, and had her do solo exercises and work out with light weights. At first, Kano taught her only the softer kata and breakfalls. After a few months, he let Yasuda engage in randori. In a year, Yasuda improved her strength and stamina so much that when she accompanied Kano and a mixed group of six men and five women on a climb to the top of Mount Fuji, she reached the summit first. Yasuda was proud of her accomplishment, but Kano did not want it to go to her head. Kano refused to give her the following day off from training. On the contrary, the training session was longer than usual, and Kano threw Yasuda over and over despite her protests of fatigue. At the end of the exhausting training session, Kano told her, "Have a hot bath and get a massage." Kano later held Yasuda up as an example of what wonders judo training can do "even for women."

Although it wasn't until 1926 that the Kodokan formally established a Women's Division, Kano had always actively encouraged women to practice judo. Among the first registered female students at the Kodokan were Ayako Akutagawa, Yasuko Morioka, and Masako Norikomi. Katsuko Kosaki was from Osaka.

Katsuko Kosaki

At the end of 1933, Katsuko Kosaki (1907–96) became the first Japanese woman black belt. Kosaki was born in Nagoya, where her family operated a fine arts gallery, with many wealthy customers, particularly famous Kabuki actors. Prior to becoming the art gallery Seigendo, it had been a Confucian academy. Since her father was more of a scholar than an art dealer, Kosaki received an excellent education. She resisted her parents' efforts to marry her off after high school graduation. One day Kosaki dropped in at a bookstore and discovered a book entitled *Judo Daigaku (Compendium of Judo)* by Takisaburo Tobari. After devouring the book, the eighteen-year-old Kosaki decided that judo was for her.

Keeping her ardor for judo secret from her parents, Kosaki found a branch dojo of the Butokukai. After some hesitation, the teacher there, named Yomeda, accepted her as a student. Following two years of training in Nagoya, Kosaki sent a letter to Tobari, the author of *Judo Daigaku*, requesting permission to become his student at his dojo in Osaka. Tobari consented, and Kosaki went to Osaka in 1929 to become his disciple.

(Takisaburo Tobari [1872–1942] was actually more of a contemporary of Kano than a student. They were fellow trainees of the Tenjin Shin'yo ryu, and then Tobari joined the Kodokan. Tobari was head of the judo division of the Butokukai in Kyoto. Tobari primarily taught and publicly demonstrated Tenjin Shin'yo ryu jujutsu rather than Kodokan judo, but he did work in close conjunction with Kano.)

During a seminar in Osaka in 1931, Kosaki was called up to act as Kano's partner for the koshiki-no-kata. During his stay in Osaka, Kano gave private instruction to Kosaki in Kodokan judo. In 1932, after Kosaki defeated three male opponents in a row, Tobari promoted her to first dan. The Kodokan certified the rank the following year. In 1933, Kosaki became the Kodokan's first female black belt.

Kosaki opened her own dojo, the Seigenkan, in 1935 in Osaka, later relocating to her hometown of Nagoya. She remained Tobari's disciple rather than Kano's, but continued to receive Kodokan ranks, second dan in 1938 and eventually fifth dan in 1981, when she was seventy-three. Kosaki is the inspiration for the popular movie and television programs called *Lady Sanshiro*, along the same lines as *Sugata Sanshiro*.

Masako Norikomi

At the 1934 kagami-biraki, Ayako Akutagawa and Yasuko Morioka were awarded first dan. Masako Norikomi was promoted to second dan at the time, skipping first dan altogether. Although few details are known about Akutagawa and Morioka, Norikomi had a long judo career.

Masako Norikomi (1913–82) was from Fukuoka Prefecture, and

A publicity still of Kano instructing Ayako Akutagawa (*left*) and Norikomi (*right*).

started practicing Kyushin ryu jujutsu when she was thirteen. In 1929, Norikomi moved to Tokyo and entered the Kodokan. Kano thought highly of Norikomi and often asked her opinion regarding the proper direction for women's judo, an appropriate ranking system, and other important issues. Norikomi was very skilled and passed through the ranks as quickly as the top men because she was as good as they were, proving it many times in matches with men. She was promoted to third dan in 1935, fourth dan in 1937, and fifth dan in 1940. Norikomi remained stuck at that rank because the Kodokan would not promote a woman above fifth dan. Finally, that unjust policy was abandoned. Norikomi was promoted to sixth dan in 1972 and seventh dan in 1982. She continued to practice judo all her life and wrote a popular textbook, *Judo for Women*, which was reprinted many times over the years.

Hisako Miyagawa

In 1936, Hisako Miyagawa (1878–1950), principal of Oin Women's College, was awarded first dan at the age of fifty-nine. She told her students, "Education must be both in mind and in body."

Keiko Fukuda

In 1934, the new Kodokan opened in Suidobashi. The family of Hachinosuke Fukuda, Kano's first teacher, was invited to attend. Later, Kano visited the Fukuda home to thank the family for their support. While he was there, he met Keiko Fukuda (b. 1913), the granddaughter of Hachinosuke. Kano encouraged the young girl to come to the Kodokan and train in the Women's Division. Fukuda did so in September 1935. The women trained every day from 3:00 P.M. to 6:00 P.M. Despite the fact that Fukuda was under five feet tall and weighed less than a hundred pounds, she displayed such an affinity for judo that her rise through the ranks was nearly as rapid as Norikomi's. Fukuda was fifth dan by 1954.

Fukuda's career thereafter is as inspiring as it is incredible. Tiny Fukuda first traveled to the United States in 1954 to hold seminars. After staying for two years, she returned to Japan. However, she was back in the States in 1966. Fukuda was so popular as an instructor that she was hired as a judo teacher at Mills College, and settled in the San Francisco area, eventually becoming an American citizen. After a letter-writing campaign to the Kodokan demanding that the ban on promoting women beyond fifth dan be lifted, Fukuda was made sixth dan in 1972. Fukuda eventually was awarded the unprecedented rank of Kodokan ninth dan and US judo tenth dan in 2006. Over the years, Fukuda has taught thousands of male and female judo students all over the world. Even with Parkinson's disease and crippling arthritis, and after a triple bypass and two heart attacks, she is, at this writing, still on the mat. Fukuda's well-known motto: "Be gentle, kind, and beautiful, yet firm and strong, both mentally and physically."

Utako Shimoda

Another amazing woman who trained with Kano is Japan's pioneer feminist Utako Shimoda (1854–1936). She was born Seki Hirao to a samurai family in Gunma Prefecture. Her parents made every effort to give her an education equal to that received by any boy. (She paid them back by sleeping naked next to their bed so the mosquitoes would bite her, not them.) The Hirao family backed the imperial faction during the civil war leading up to the Meiji Restoration and was thus rewarded with employment in the new government. The father was called to Tokyo in 1868, and the family followed in 1870. Seki was a brilliant student and such a good poet that the empress changed Seki's name to Utako, "the nymph that sings beautifully."

After marrying the swordsman Takeo Shimoda, Utako resigned her office in the imperial household. Her husband fell ill, however, so Shimoda was obliged to open a private school at her home. Since nearly all of the wives of the ex–samurai officials in the new government were former geisha or courtesans, Shimoda tutored them in the Chinese classics and poetry composition.

In 1884, Takeo died and Shimoda began her career as a professional educator. She became a professor and then principal of the newly established Girls' Peer School. (Kano's future wife, Sumako Takezoe, was a student there later.) From 1893 to 1895, Shimoda spent two years in Europe and the United States studying the local educational systems. In the United States, Shimoda was shocked to find boys and girls being educated together in the same classroom. She also was surprised at the widespread inclusion of physical education as an essential part of the curriculum. When Shimoda returned to Japan, she reported in no uncertain terms: "Japan will never go anywhere as a nation unless men and women receive an equal education."

Shimoda argued that the reason the countries of Asia were weak compared to the Western powers lay in the fact that they had not developed education for women. This included physical education as well. She said, "Weak women, weak men." Shi-

Utako Shimoda (1854–1936), Kano's female counterpart—martial artist, educator, writer, internationalist, and political force.

moda wanted to educate both Japanese and Chinese women according to her standards. The Practical Women's School (Jissen Jogakko) that Shimoda established in 1899 was as much for Chinese female exchange students as for native Japanese women.

Shimoda practiced with Kano one-to-one in the earliest days of the Kodokan. Since Shimoda was raised in a samurai household, she had a good knowledge of the martial arts. Six years older than Kano, just as smart and as well educated, and supremely self-confident, she was no rank beginner. Shimoda was Kano's equal in many ways. Their training sessions must have been spirited. Shimoda and Kano had a lot in common, both as martial artists and as educators. In many ways, Kano and Shimoda are responsible for the establishment of modern coeducation in Japan. They were quite a pair.

Shimoda continued her battle for women's rights up to the end of her long and eventful life. Like Kano, Shimoda was tireless. She founded three women's schools and wrote dozens of books on education, politics, physical culture, and literature, all the while composing poetry. Unlike Kano, she had to deal with male chauvinism. A newspaper once ran a critical series on her with the theme "The Vamp Utako Shimoda." Shimoda died in 1936, two years before Kano, at age eighty-two.

Kano and His Students   177

Kano's Chinese Students

While Kano had many illustrious Japanese students, a number of the Chinese students who studied at the Kobun Gakuen or the Tokyo Teacher Training College became pivotal figures in modern Chinese history. Kano's daughter Noriko recalled that her father was deeply involved with the Kobun Gakuen and its students, spending almost as much time on directing the school as on the Kodokan. Kano felt that the only way China could progress was through education. Since the connection of Kano to the Chinese students of the Kobun Gakuen is barely recognized, it needs to be highlighted here.

Lu Xun

Lu Xun (known as Rojin in Japanese, 1881–1936) is revered in both China and Japan as a master of modern literature. Lu Xun was born in Shaoxing into a family of scholars. On a government scholarship, Lu Xun went to Japan in 1902, where he enrolled in Kano's Kobun Gakuen. As mentioned, there was a dojo at the school, and Lu Xun practiced Kodokan judo for a year. He returned to China in 1903, and then came back to Japan in 1904 to study medicine at Sendai Medical School. Since Lu Xun was more interested in literature than medicine, he left Sendai in 1906 to go to Tokyo, where he began his career as a writer.

During the next three years in Tokyo, Lu Xun wrote essays in classical Chinese on various topics and did translations of European literature. In 1909, Lu Xun returned to China and began a parallel career as an educator. While teaching at a number of different schools and working at the newly established Ministry of Education—he was a lot like Kano in this regard—Lu Xun produced a huge output of short stories, essays, literary criticism, social commentary, works of history, dictionaries, and translations. Lu Xun revolutionized Chinese literature. (Among his works available in English translation are *Diary of a Madman*, *Selected Stories*, and *True Story of Ah Q*.)

Although Lu Xun never joined the Communist Party—he

was made an honorary member after his death—Mao Zedong considered him a hero and wrote the inscriptions on Lu Xun's tomb. Fittingly, as a man honored in both countries, Lu Xun's works have appeared in both Japanese and Chinese school textbooks.

Huang Xing

A revolutionary of a different type was Huang Xing (1874–1916), known as the "Eight-Fingered General." Huang Xing was from Huan. He was a clever student and, like Lu Xun, received a government scholarship to study at Kano's Kobun Gakuen in 1902. While there, Huang Xing spent his time practicing judo and privately learning military science from a retired Japanese officer. Huang Xing was said to have practiced horsemanship and marksmanship every morning before school.

The rest of Huang Xing's life was devoted to the Xinhai Revolution in China. He traveled back and forth between China and Japan, organizing and participating in several revolts. Huang Xing teamed up with Sun Yat-sen in Japan, and thereafter served as his commander in chief in China. Huang Xing was a hero of the Wuchang Uprising in 1911, which led to the overthrow of the Qing dynasty.

Huang Xing became the military leader of the Kuomintang when it was established in 1912. More battles followed, and Huang Xing died with his boots on in 1916. He was forty-two.

Qiu Jin

Another even fiercer revolutionary was Qiu Jin (1875–1907), called "Woman Warrior of Mirror Lake." From an early age, the rebellious Qiu Jin displayed a remarkable talent for poetry and the martial arts. She memorized the classics of Chinese poetry as well as learning how to fight with a sword, shoot a rifle, ride horseback, and run for miles.

In 1896, Qiu Jin married and moved to Beijing. She had two children, but her husband was a drunk. She abandoned the family and in 1904 went to Japan to study. Qiu Jin entered Kano's

Kobun Gakuen, and then Shimoda's Practical Women's School. Although Qiu Jin was supposed to be studying education, crafts, and nursing, just like Huang Xing she mostly practiced martial arts—judo, shooting, and making explosives—and engaged in revolutionary activities. All the time she was in Japan, she organized protests against both the Chinese and Japanese governments, tirelessly campaigning for women's rights.

Qiu Jin eventually returned to China, where her revolutionary activities continued unabated. She joined or organized secret societies dedicated to the overthrow of the Manchu dynasty. Qiu Jin was as radical a feminist as can be imagined, demanding a woman's right to freely marry, be educated, engage in any occupation of her choosing, and enjoy complete equality with men. Qiu Jin was an Asian Joan of Arc. In one picture we have of her, a defiant Qiu Jin stares straight at the camera holding a dagger. She was a cross-dresser, appearing more frequently in men's clothes than women's to make the point that the sexes were on equal terms.

The school she headed was supposed to be a sports academy; it was actually a training ground for revolutionaries. As a result of such provocative and vocal agitation, Qiu Jin was arrested by the government in 1907 as a plotter of armed insurrection. Qiu Jin was tortured and then publicly beheaded. She has become a heroine and martyr to the cause of women's liberation.

Yang Changji

Yang Changji (1871–1920) studied at the Kobunkan English Academy and then the Tokyo Teacher Training College. After graduating from the college in 1907, he studied philosophy in Scotland. In 1913, Yang Changji became a teacher of ethics and education at Hunan First Teachers College. Yang Changji was the favorite teacher of Mao Zedong, who was a student there. Yang Changji is known as the "Man Who Molded Mao Zedong." Yang Changji introduced Mao to Kano's ideas; in 1917, Mao wrote a paper, "Research on Physical Education," based on Kano's educational theories, that appeared in the journal *Xing Qing Nian*.

Yang Changji was Mao's early mentor, patron, and father-in-law. Mao accompanied Yang Changij when he moved to Beijing to teach at the university. Mao lived with Yang Changji, who got Mao a job at the university library. Mao and Yang Changji's daughter Kaihui became lovers. They married after Yang Changji died of illness in 1920. Kaihui raised their three children, all the while engaged in revolutionary activities, particularly peasant movements. She hardly saw Mao during much of their marriage—he essentially abandoned her—but supported his efforts on the front, and continued to write him love letters, often in the form of poetry. In 1930, Kaihui was arrested by one of Mao's enemies, a Kuomindang warlord. She was tortured and then shot to death, in front of one of her sons, professing her devotion to Mao and his cause to the end.

Chen Duxiu

Chen Duxiu (1879–1942), cofounder of the Chinese Communist Party, together with Li Dazhao (1888–1927) in 1921, studied the Japanese language at the Kobun Gakuen for half a year or so, but he was primarily a cadet at the Seijo Military Academy during his stay in Japan from 1901 to 1908. Chen Duxiu helped found the Communist Party, and was its undisputed leader until 1927. However, he was expelled from the party in 1929 and was on the outs with Mao and other members of the Comintern for the rest of his life. In 1932, he was arrested and imprisoned by the Nationalist government. After his release from prison in 1937, Chen Duxiu faded into obscurity and died in 1942.

Chen Duxiu was a prolific and provocative journalist and theoretician who left a huge corpus of work. In many ways, he can be considered the father of modern Chinese journalism. Recently at home and abroad, there has been a renewed interest in Chen Duxiu's writings.

Yang Du

Unlike nearly all of the students at the Kobunkan English Academy who were revolutionaries, Yang Du (1875–1931) was a conservative who supported the establishment of a provisional government around the imperial system. (Yang Du was a student at the Kobun Gakuen in 1902.) He clashed publicly with Kano and the radical Chinese exchange students about the current government and its role in the future of education in China. Yang Du made an about-face later in life, becoming a member of the Communist Party in 1928. While Yang Du remained active as a politician, he also became a serious scholar of Chan (Zen) Buddhism. One of Yang Du's pen names was "Chan Master Tiger." Yang Du also tried to make it as a professional painter near the end of his life. He died in Shanghai at the age of fifty-six.

Chen Tianhua

Firebrand Chen Tianhua (1875–1905) was the most extreme radical of the Chinese exchange students at the Kobun Gakuen, where he studied for seven months. He railed against everything that the Chinese, Japanese, and Russian governments did. Chen Tianhua wrote protest letters in his own blood and called for armed insurrections everywhere in Asia. Chen Tianhua's militancy consumed him: as a protest against the actions of the Japanese government, Chen Tianhua committed suicide in 1905 by throwing himself into Tokyo Bay.

Hu Hanmin

Hu Hanmin (1879–1936), a right-winger and fervent anti-Communist, was at the Kobun Gakuen in 1902. Hu Hanmin was a close associate of Sun Yat-sen, and a leading member of the Kuomintang, serving as premier of the party from 1925 to 1931. Hu Hanmin and Chiang Kai-shek were engaged in a long power struggle for control of the Kuomintang that only ended with Hu's death in 1936.

Chen Yinke

Chen Yinke (1890–1969), a student at the Kobun Gakuen between 1902 and 1905, was not a politician of any persuasion. Chen Yinke devoted his life to scholarship, not revolution. After leaving Japan, Chen Yinke later got scholarships to study at Humboldt

University in Berlin, the University of Zurich, Institut d'Études Politiques de Paris, and Harvard University. Chen Yinke mastered many Eastern and Western languages, including Mongolian, Tibetan, Manchu, Japanese, Sanskrit, Pali, Persian, Turkic, Tangut, English, French, German, Latin, and Greek. His research interests were just as broad, ranging from Buddhist texts in Sanskrit, Pali, Chinese, Mongol, and Tibetan to his best-known and most important work, a study of Liu Rushi (1618–64), poet, courtesan, and consort of the Ming scholar Qian Qianyi (1582–1664). Chin Yinke served as professor at a number of major universities and was elected a member of the Academia Sinica.

Chen Yinke, the "professor of professors," possessed a prodigious intellect. His scholarship was vast, deep, challenging, and provocative. Since Chen Yinke went completely blind later in life, he required assistants to help with his research by tracking down material, reading texts to him aloud, and taking down his words for publication verbatim. Much of Chen Yinke's final work was based on his precise memory of a vast corpus of literature. His books were composed not on paper but in his head.

Chen Yinke longed to stay out of politics altogether, resisting any attempt to harness his scholarship for the Communist cause or alter his writings to reflect Marxist interpretation of history. Consequently, the blind and frail Chen Yinke was badly treated in the late 1950s and 1960s by the Communist Party and then by barbaric Red Guards during the Cultural Revolution. Chen Yinke's works went unpublished, former students and colleagues turned against him, his salary was frozen, his library looted, and his manuscripts burned. Chen Yinke died in 1969.

However, Chen Yinke's scholarship managed to survive. His voluminous works began appearing in print in 1980, and he has taken his place in the pantheon of great Chinese savants.

Li Shucheng

Li Shucheng (1882–1965) was at the Kobun Gakuen from 1902 to 1903 and later studied military science at the Tokyo Army Academy. Li Shucheng was a general for the Kuomintang, and the initial meeting of the National Congress of the Chinese Communist Party was held at his house in Shanghai in 1921. Following the end of World War II, Li Shucheng tried to no avail to negotiate peace between the Communists and the Kuomintang. Upon the establishment of the People's Republic of China (PRC) in 1949, Li Shucheng became minister of agriculture.

Sun Qichang

Sun Qichang (1885–1954) graduated from the Tokyo Teacher Training College. After returning to Japan, Sun Qichang became principal of the Mukden Commercial High School. He then became involved in the politics of northern China, becoming an official in the Beiyang government. The Beiyang "warlord" government agitated for an independent state in Manchuria. In 1932, with Japanese collusion, the State of Manchukuo was established.

Sun Qichang was a senior official in the Manchukuo government serving as Finance Minister and Minsiter of Civil Affairs. In 1942, he was forced to resign from the government over disagreements regarding economic policy. Following the invasion of the Soviet army and the collapse of the Manchukuo state in 1945, he went into hiding. He was eventually discovered by agents of the People's Republic of China in 1951 and was executed in 1954.

In 1938, Sun Qichang composed a long message of condolence for Kano's funeral. In his commomeration of Kano, he praised Kano's career as an educator and founder of Kodokan judo. He wrote that Kano's philoshophy of *seiryoku zenyo, jita kyoei* had universal application and also mentioned Kano's love and concern for China. He concluded, "Kano Sensei left this world as a great being, a high priest, a living Buddha."

Lin Boqu

Lin Boqu (1886–1960), who studied at the Kobunkan English Academy from 1904 to 1905, became a founding member of the Communist Party. Lin Boqu was in exile in the Soviet Union from 1928 to 1932. He participated in the Long March and, in 1949, was appointed general secretary of the Politburo. Lin Boqu was included in the famous oil painting *Founding Ceremony of the Nation* by Dong Xiwen (1914–73), unveiled in 1953. Later, however, Lin Boqu was painted out at the order of the Red Guards. Happily, in 1979, his memory was rehabilitated, and he was painted back in. (Depending on who was in power, figures in the painting were continually being removed and restored; the painting was revised four times.)

Fan Yuanlian

Fan Yuanlian (1874–1927) was a student at the Tokyo Teacher Training College from 1900 to 1904. He was an educator who became president of Beijing Teachers College in 1923, and later chairman of the Chinese Education and Culture Committee. Fan Yuanlian visited Europe and the United States several times to study educational institutions there and is considered one of the founders of China's university system.

Tian Han

The playwright Tian Han (1898–1968) was in Japan later than the other Chinese exchange students. He studied at the Tokyo Teacher Training College from 1917 to 1920. After his return to China, Tian Han went on to write many famous plays, in both the traditional Chinese opera and modern drama modes. He also did movie screenplays. Tian Han, who joined the Communist Party in 1932, is best known for composing the lyrics to the People's Republic of China's national anthem, "March of the Volunteers," in 1934. Nie Er (1912–35) set the lyrics to music while living in Japan. (Nie Er drowned in a swimming accident soon after he composed the music for the anthem.)

Similarly to the *Founding Ceremony of the Nation* painting, "March of the Volunteers" suffered alteration over the years. After some controversy regarding the lyrics, "March of the Volunteers" became the regional national anthem in 1949 at the founding of the People's Republic of China. Later, Tian Han was imprisoned by the Red Guards for his historical drama *Xie Yaohuan*, which was thought to be a veiled criticism of Mao. Playing of "March of the Volunteers" was banned, and Tian Han died in prison in 1968. The anthem was restored in 1969 with new lyrics praising Mao and the heroes of the Long March. Many people kept singing the old version, however. In 1982, references to Mao were cut out and the original lyrics of 1934 restored. "March of the Volunteers" was officially made the national anthem of the PRC in 2004. Tian Han was rehabilitated posthumously in 1979.

In addition to the Chinese students who studied at Kano's academic institutions, there were Koreans who trained at the Kodokan as early as 1901. A Korean Division of the Kodokan was established in 1918. Unfortunately, not much is known about the Korean members who practiced there—alas, this is always the case because the Koreans were largely dismissed by both the Chinese and the Japanese—but it is known that Yi Son-gi (1893–1971) was open tournament champion for his age division in Japan in 1932, 1937, and 1938. He returned to Korea and established Kodokan judo in his native country. He was awarded ninth dan by the Korean Judo Association in 1965.

Two Indian nationals, G. N. Potolen and S. R. Miha, entered the Kodokan in 1904.

Kano's First Generation of Western Students

It has always been a matter of keen interest among Western students of judo to somehow determine who was "Kano's first non-Asian student at the Kodokan." Part of this desire is to establish "bragging rights" for a particular nationality. At any rate, here is an outline of what is known so far.

Since the Reverend T. Lindsay delivered a paper on judo with Kano in 1888, it is not out of the question that he was Kano's first Caucasian student, but there is no record of his actually being enrolled at the Kodokan. The first non-Japanese in the Kodokan records, and also mentioned by Kano, is the British military man H. M. Hughes, listed as a trainee in 1893. Hughes evidently did not receive rank. The Eastlake brothers from the United States were at the Kodokan a bit later. The elder, F. Washington Eastlake (1858–1905), who weighed well over two hundred pounds, was an English teacher; the younger, a trading house employee, was smaller. They did not last long—perhaps because big brother Eastlake grew tired of the embarrassment of being tossed around by much smaller men. At any rate, their interest in Kodokan judo was primarily for its principles, not the technical side.

In 1889, they were succeeded by Professor Land from Princeton University, who spent ten months of serious training at the Kodokan. Two other Americans, John Forbes Perkins and John Wells Farley, are listed in the 1889 register. There is a John Wells Farley (1878–1959) who was head coach of the University of Maine football team (1901 and 1903) and the Harvard football team (1902). He was from Boston and could very well have been one of the many Bostonians who visited Japan during the Meiji period.

Perhaps the first European to receive a first dan rank was the Italian naval man Carlo Oletti. Since the Italian ambassador Martino had attended a demonstration at the Kodokan in 1890, he likely told his countrymen about judo. Oletti was with a group of Italian sailors who were sent to the Kodokan to train in 1905. Oletti received first dan in 1908 and went on to become the father of Italian judo. Kano visited Oletti's dojos in Italy in 1928 and 1934. David T. Weed, a half-Japanese American who spent all of his life in Japan, was promoted to first dan in 1910, and to second dan in 1912. Weed's teacher was Kunisaburo Iizuka.

In 1911, the colorful English journalist E. J. Harrison (1873–1961) attained first dan. His book *Fighting Spirit in Japan*, published in 1912, is a highly entertaining account of his adventures at the Kodokan and elsewhere. Over the years, Harrison published a number of books on judo and the martial arts, and he was active on the judo scene in London. Harrison married the sister of A. J. Ross (1893–1971). The Ross family was living in Japan at the time, and A.J. started training at the Kodokan when he was a teenager, probably around 1907. Ross obtained at least first dan while he was there, although the year is not known. In 1928, he founded the first Australian judo dojo in Brisbane.

The Englishman W. E. Steers was awarded first dan in 1912. Kano described Steers as his most earnest foreign student. Steers literally gave up everything to study judo, selling his London home and moving to Japan to train full-time at the Kodokan. He was already in his midfifties at the time, so Kano gave Steers personal instruction, perhaps to spare him some of the wear and tear he would have received at the hands of the younger judo men.

The Russian V. S. Oshchepkov (1898–1937) entered the Kodokan as a thirteen-year-old boy in 1911. He earned his first dan in 1913 and his second dan in 1917. He had seen judo demonstrated by Takeo Hirose in Russia. Oshchepkov was a mysterious figure, a spy, and very skilled at the martial arts. In Russia, he taught a system of hand-to-hand combat and bayonet fighting based on Kodokan judo, elements from other combat arts, and, no doubt, broad personal experience. Oshchepkov was also instrumental in the development of the Russian-style judo called *sambo*. Oshchepkov served as a commander in the Red Army, training soldiers and continuing his activities as a spy in China. During the Stalinist purge, Oshchepkov was accused of being a double agent, working covertly with the Japanese, imprisoned, and then executed in 1937.

Scotsman Alan Smith, another military man, attained first dan in January 1916 and wore his kilt to receive his certificate from Kano. Somehow Smith got to the United States and quickly became a captain in the US Army, serving as a hand-to-hand combat trainer. There is a military training film, evidently made in 1917, that features Smith and lists him as "3 dan Kano Ryu Jiujitsu," which of course is impossible (at least at that time), since he was only awarded first dan the year before. In his travel diary of 1920, Kano mentioned meeting Smith in New York, describing him as second dan and an enthusiastic promoter of Kodokan judo. Smith wrote a textbook entitled *Jujutsu: A Complete Course of Self-Defense* that was published in 1920. In it, there is this bit of judo wisdom that Smith got from a Japanese instructor: "A hundred tricks are easy to learn, but the one principle behind them takes years to master." Smith's whereabouts are unknown after 1920. Maybe he was a spy too.

In 1922, a Norwegian diplomat named Laurit Gronvold began training at the Kodokan. He was formally awarded first dan six years later, reportedly in the presence of the emperor, likely at an event for foreign diplomats.

Moshe Feldenkrais (1904–84), founder of the Feldenkrais Method, began practicing jujutsu on his own in Palestine and later in France. In 1933, Feldenkrais finagled a meeting with Kano, who was in France as a guest of the French government. Kano's version of the meeting is low-key:

> We met in my hotel room. He showed me a manual on jujutsu that he had written in Hebrew. I pointed out the mistakes. He didn't think that they were mistakes. I demonstrated the correct form of a choke hold on him. He gave up. He wanted me to correct the entire manuscript. I replied that I did not have time to do so, but made three or four comments. (Synopsis of the encounter in *Mind over Muscle*, pp. 47–50).

In contrast, Feldenkrias's own account is livelier, as shown in the following summary:

> In my book, there was a demonstration of a knife-disarming attack. Kano was impressed. "I've never seen anything like this." Regarding my choke-hold techniques, however, Kano said they were not good. "What do you mean no good? Get out of this!" I applied the hold, gently at first because he was an old man, and then with full force when it did not work. Suddenly, I saw black. I was completely out. When I came to, he let me try it again. Same result—but I realized that he had used my strength to strangle me. I finally understood what judo is all about. (The whole story appears in "Interview with Moshe," *SemioPhysics*, 1977, pp. 7–14).

Feldenkrais, a boastful, bombastic, tireless self-promoter, claimed that he and Kano became good friends after that and corresponded regularly, but that seems unlikely given the differences in age and status. At any rate, Feldenkrais earned second dan by 1938, and published a couple of judo textbooks. Judo heavily influenced the development of his Feldenkrais Method.

The first non-Japanese woman Kodokan first dan was Sarah Mayer. She began the practice of judo in London and then spent two years, 1934–35, studying at the Kodokan. Since Mayer considered the Women's Division of the Kodokan little more than a "finishing school for young Japanese ladies," she trained mostly with the men. She met Kano a few times, and described him as "a charming old gentleman with European manners." She also noted that at certain times he looked quite sickly, and that many of his students thought he might not live much longer. (This was in 1934, four years before Kano's death; he was obviously getting run-down.) Mayer obtained first dan in 1935.

From these examples of his interaction with students from all parts of the world, we can see that Kano was a great educator, leader, and statesman, whose influence on twentieth-century society was pervasive.

5

The Teachings of Jigoro Kano

◉

IT MAY COME AS A SURPRISE that the favorite saying of the dignified grand master of Kodokan judo and principal of the Tokyo Teacher Training College was literally "What is this shit!" (*Nani kuso*). By this, Kano was saying to his students, "Shit happens. Deal with it!"

Kano lived in a time of tremendous social upheaval, war, political uncertainty, economic depression, assassinations, labor strikes and riots, agitation for human rights, and international intrigue. Just about the deepest shit there is.

Throughout his life, Kano confronted all those difficulties and more, never recoiling from any challenge or avoiding it. Challenges in life need to be handled decisively and directly. By *Nani kuso*, Kano meant, "Whatever occurs, no matter how difficult the situation in which you find yourself, don't let it defeat you! Use judo principles, and every obstacle can be overcome. Unprecedented crisis sparks unlimited opportunities."

Kano established these basic precepts for training:

1. Trainees in judo are here to forge their body and mind while working for the greater good of society.
2. Always bow toward the master's seat when entering or leaving the dojo.
3. Respect must be shown to the master, instructors, your seniors, and to all the other trainees. Seniors must look after

their juniors, and juniors should listen to the advice of the seniors.

4. Training is never to be skipped except in the event of serious illness or injury. Inform the instructor beforehand if you must be absent for any reason.
5. Casual or sloppy attire is not permitted.
6. Proper posture must be maintained at all times. Informal sitting, standing, or lying in the dojo is not allowed.
7. Never enter the dojo or engage in training when intoxicated.
8. Being unclothed, changing, or smoking outside the changing room is not allowed. Clothes and personal belongings must be kept in the changing room.
9. Participate as much as possible in all dojo events—New Year's ceremony, monthly contests, and the twice-yearly Kohaku tournaments.
10. Through judo training, cultivate sincerity, morality, proper deportment, good physical and mental health, and a positive attitude.

(Compiled from the journal *Shugyosha kokoroe*, March 1894 and May 1912)

Kano taught these principles to his students:

Do not let victory enthrall you.

Do not let defeat defeat you.

When it is safe, do not be careless.

When it is dangerous, do not be afraid.

Above all, move forward on your path to the end.

In order to defeat the enemy without, you must defeat the enemy within.

Further, he established the Five Principles of Judo:

1. Carefully observe yourself and your situation, others, and the environment.
2. Seize the initiative in whatever you undertake.
3. Consider fully, act decisively.
4. Know when to stop.
5. Keep to the middle.

Regarding the first principle, Kano elaborated:

> Prior to a match, you must take into account the physique, strength, and level of skill of your opponent. You need to carefully observe his character. As well as gathering as much information as you can about your opponent, you must observe the environment in which you are situated—the people who are around, the walls, possible obstacles, and the like. Taking all this into consideration will make you much more effective in the contest. The same approach holds true in business, politics, and education.

Kano was captivated by the phrase "Soft can control the hard" (*Ju yoku go o seisuru*, 柔能剛制). That quote comes from the second century B.C.E. Chinese military manual *Three Strategies of Huang Shi Gong* (Upper Strategy). The entire quote is:

> Soft can control the hard; weak can control strong. Being soft at the right time is a virtue; being hard at the wrong time is a disaster.

That principle became the pivot of Kano's philosophy of life. Ju (柔) has many different connotations: "soft," "yielding," "pliant," and "flexible yet unbreakable." Kano's original quest in jujutsu was to discover exactly what the concept of ju was in actual physical terms and practical application. He found ju when he was finally able to throw his teacher Iikubo. That was the physical ju, the *kuzushi*, "off balancing." As soon as Kano discovered how to off-balance his opponent, using subtle but extremely effective timing, it was comparatively simple to throw him in any of the eight directions.

Kuzushi is the key to all judo throws. However, kuzushi has to be applied with precise *tsukuri* (positioning) and *kake* (execution). As Kano discovered, if one's kuzushi, tsukuri, and kake are perfect, the opponent essentially throws himself. Mastering kuzushi was Kano's judo enlightenment. It was true ju.

The next question for Kano was the wider implications of ju. Utilizing ju in order to win over an opponent in a match is superficial; for Kano, the principle of ju was of limited value if it could not be applied to one's daily life and then to society as a whole.

Kano's mastery of kuzushi and ju enabled him to build the two pillars of his philosophy: *seiryoku zenyo* (精力善用), "focused effort, maximum efficiency"; and *jita kyoei* (自他共栄), "mutual well-being and benefit."

Seiryoku zenyo, jita kyoei was Kano's mantra, a kind of judo elixir meant to cure all ailments, individual and social. The principle of concentrated effort, maximum efficiency can be applied to any endeavor. Kano first became aware of how well seiryoku zenyo worked during his student days. A classmate named Shiraishi always got good grades despite the fact that he never crammed like other students. Kano wanted to know why. Kano noticed that whenever a class ended early or was canceled, Shiraishi used the time to study and prepare his homework. During school, Shiraishi wasted not a minute of time by chatting or fooling around with fellow students. For Shiraishi, school time was study time, nothing else. (While admirable, it must be said that only one out of a hundred students will ever act like Shiraishi.)

In judo, the first goal is to develop self-control and self-cultivation, best realized through seiryoku zenyo. Kano believed that the effectiveness of seiryoku zenyo could be evaluated most clearly in the laboratory (the dojo). The execution of a technique provides immediate feedback—if it worked or why it did not work. The understanding of seiryoku zenyo fostered in the dojo leads to its application in all aspects of daily life. Seiryoku zenyo should be the guiding principle for how one thinks, talks, eats, dresses, walks, works, plays, and relates to others. "Don't waste anything. Use it efficiently" is common sense, but Kano extended the concept of seiryoku zenyo to speech: "Complaining, arguing, gossiping, and the like are all a great waste of time and energy." And thinking: "Worry, anger, bearing grudges, and other such negative emotions drain away valuable hours that could be better spent on positive thinking."

Kano had this to say about seiryoku zenyo:

> Powerful people clear forests, build roads, and construct villages; those with less physical energy plant and gather vegetables, make clothes, and care for others. Neither group is "stronger" than the other. They both have their appropriate strengths.

It must be said that Kano had impossibly high hopes for seiryoku zenyo. As mentioned, Kano seriously believed that seiryoku zenyo is a remedy for anything. Seiryoku zenyo is a good guideline—following the principle himself allowed Kano to accomplish so much—but no one is going to weigh every decision in life according to whether or not it is an iota more efficient than another choice. Seiryoku zenyo was wonderful in principle, but very difficult to follow in every facet of life. For example, Kano complained that there were too many restaurants and pubs in Japan because such establishments encouraged people to waste too much time eating and drinking. However, most people need to kick back once in a while, have a nice meal or a relaxing drink, or simply smell the flowers. Kano was relentlessly industrious.

Jita kyoei, on the other hand, has practical application on a broader scale. Doing things in a manner that benefits oneself and others naturally makes everyone prosper.

The embodiment of Kano's jita kyoei theory was his hero Harunori Uesugi (1751–1822), ninth head of the Yonezawa Domain. In order to pull the domain out of its crushing debt, Uesugi cut his retainers' incomes to one-sixth of the previous amount and reduced his own living expenses from 1,500 ryo to 209 ryo a year. The number of maidservants in his castle went from fifty to nine. Uesugi wore cloth, not silk. He ate one meal a day consisting of soup and vegetables. Uesugi reopened the clan school, built a medical college, and invited the best scholars from Edo to teach at the institutions. He made his retainers and samurai dig ditches and build dikes for irrigation of the domain's rice fields. He supported the old industries and started new ones. Promotions in the domain government were based on merit. Kano was fond of holding Uesugi up as an example to his students:

> Whenever Uesugi traveled in his domain, he gave a strict command for his attendants not to let their horses damage any fields along the way. Uesugi was always careful himself not to step on plants when he was inspecting the fields of the farmers in his domain. Once when an attendant accidentally damaged some rice stalks, Uesugi made him go to the farmer and pay a fine. Uesugi considered every grain of rice, every piece of paper, every bit of cloth, to be precious because of the great amount of effort that had been put into growing or making it. Uesugi wanted nothing produced by the hard work of the people in the domain to be wasted. Everyone in his domain should share in the work, and everyone should share the benefits. We need to have the same attitude as Uesugi today.

Similarly, Kano believed that in a system based on jita kyoei, capitalism and socialism could actually work hand in hand to develop the best possible economic framework for society. Even though such ideals are clearly based on traditional Japanese values, in the 1930s there was a faction in the Japanese military that demanded Kano resign from the Kodokan on the grounds that jita kyoei was Communist propaganda!

In Kano's world, there was nothing but strife: between owners and workers, between politicians left and right, between upper and lower social classes, and between nations East and West.

Wherever he was, Kano tirelessly promoted seiryoku zenyo, jita kyoei in the hope that his ceaseless preaching on the brotherhood of man and the world's interdependence would have an effect. The message of Kano's Kodokan judo was meant to be universal, free of political, national, racial, economic, or religious taint.

Although the last thing Kano would consider himself is a Zen philosopher, for many years there was a huge signboard displayed above the main stage of the Kodokan brushed by Katsu Kaishu describing his impressions of judo:

With no mind, naturally enter marvelous activity;
With no effort, manifest unlimited magic movement.

No mind (*mushin*) is the highest stage of Zen enlightenment. No effort (*mui*) is the heart of Taoist philosophy. Both elements are in Kodokan judo.

Kano's Teachings Expressed in Calligraphy

I have always maintained that the best way to get a true idea of what principles a master holds most dear is to study his or her calligraphy. Written works and recorded lectures contain a teacher's ideas, of course, but no matter who it is, written works quickly become dated, even obsolete. And, honestly, many texts are tedious to begin with. In stark contrast, calligraphic statements must be short, direct, right to the point. The words and phrases have to capture the essence of the master's teachings. In addition, there is the proverb in East Asia that "calligraphy reveals the person." The brushwork reveals what is in the calligrapher's heart.

After Kodokan judo and education, Kano's passion was the practice of calligraphy. As mentioned, when Kano was a pupil at the Ubukata Academy, he was required to turn in three notebooks of practice brushwork every day. Ubukata, a highly respected calligrapher, drilled Kano in the basics of calligraphy.

At home, Kano used newspaper to practice his brushwork, usually chatting with his wife as he did so, until the paper was completely black. When the family moved to a bigger place, Kano had a room set aside for calligraphy. In his lifetime, Kano brushed thousands of pieces of calligraphy for his friends, his students, and for display in dojos and institutions of learning. Kano never turned down a request for his brushwork, no matter how busy he was. On occasion, he even brushed requests for calligraphy in the stationmaster's office while waiting for a train. The last night Kano was at the Kodokan, he worked till morning brushing a mountain of promised calligraphy. There is a saying, "Master calligraphers do not brush many formal pieces," the reasoning being that too many pieces will lessen the value, in terms of both price and appreciation. When told that by other professors, Kano replied with a laugh, "I think of my calligraphy as a textbook. I want everyone to have a piece of my brushwork."

Up until about the age of sixty, Kano used the pen name *Konan* (甲南). *Konan* is a reference to Kano's birthplace, meaning "South of the Rokko Mountains." In his sixties, Kano switched to *Shinkosai* (進乎斎). This is a reference to the Taoist butcher mentioned in book three of Zhuangzi (Chuang-tzu):

> The emperor noticed that whenever his butcher cut up meat, the meat seemed to fall apart by itself. It looked as if the butcher was not slicing anything at all. He asked the butcher the secret of his art. The butcher replied, "By following the Tao, not the technique. I have learned to let the knife follow the natural lines of the meat, thus meeting no resistance. The knife of an ordinary butcher needs to be changed every month. A good butcher can use his knife for three years. My knife has been in use for nineteen years."

Shinkosai means, "To follow the Way [of judo], not the technique [of judo]."

Kiissai (帰一斎) was Kano's pen name when he was in his seventies. The Chinese philosopher Xun Zi said, "Kings all have different methods of ruling, but the one basic principle is the same." Near the end of his busy and eventful life, Kano felt he needed to return to the one principle—the Way of ju.

Kano composed few poems. His calligraphy consisted of quotes from the Chinese classics, a few Zen phrases, and personal mottoes. His student Muneo Shiotani compiled a list of framed Kano calligraphies in dojos and schools across Japan. Here's what he found in terms of frequency:

1. *Jundo Seisho* (順道制勝). "Following the Way Produces Victory." *Jundo* is a Confucian concept meaning "proper behavior," "maintain high principles," and "to follow the natural course of things." In judo, *seisho* means "obtain victory" and "emerge victorious." In education, *seisho* means "achieve the goal" and "realize great results." With eighty-one examples, this was by far the most common calligraphy on display.

   Jundo Seisho has a second verse that Kano added on occasion: *Gyofu Gaijin* (行不害人, "The Best Behavior Harms No One").

2. *Seiryoku Zenyo* (精力善用). "Concentrated Effort, Maximum Efficiency." Number two at sixty-six examples.

3. *Riki Hittasu* (力必達). "Effort Ensures Results." Another interpretation would be "Strive and You Will Arrive." Twenty-one examples.

4. *Shinjin Jizai* (心身自在). "Mind and Body Perfectly Free." *Jizai* means "freely" and "with perfect ease." "Mind and Body Perfectly Free" is what we should strive for in our training and studies. It is an enlightened state of being where what one thinks, says, and does are in accord. Twelve examples.

5. *Jinryoku* (尽力). "Exhaustive Effort." Eleven examples.

6. *Joko Ekise* (成己益世). "Perfect Yourself, Benefit Society." If you want to make the world better, make yourself better. Eight examples.

7. *Zenryoku Saizen Katsudo* (精力最善活用). "Employ Concentrated Effort, Maximum Effect in Every Pursuit." Five examples.

8. *Jita Kyoei* (自他共栄). "Mutual Well-being and Benefit." Five examples.
9. *Ketsuko Ketsujo* (竭己竭成). "Give It Your All to Accomplish All." Five examples.
10. *Shuko Chijin* (修己治人). "Self-Development Makes the Ideal Citizen." This sentiment is the heart of Confucianism. The more people cultivate their minds, the better citizens they will be. Five examples.

Here are some other favorite themes Kano used for his calligraphy, in order based on the number of characters in each verse.

Tando (探道). Search for the Way.

Wakei (和敬). Harmony and Respect.

Waku (和煦). Harmony and Warmth.

Wakyo (和協). Harmony and Cooperation.

Ryuho (流芳). Leave Your Mark (on future generations). Literally, "Let your fragrance flow."

Renketsu (廉潔). Integrity.

Jinki (盡己). Exhaust Yourself. (Make Every Effort.)

Kinzeraku (勤是楽). Movement Is Bliss.

Gabogo (我忘吾). Forget about Yourself.

Zenshokyu (善処窮). Find the Best Place to Be.

Jinki Shisei (盡己竢成). Great Effort, Great Result.

Teisho Jidan (抵掌而談). Persuasion over Aggression.

Wachu Kyodo (和衷協同). Harmony Works Wonders.

Shinjin Mumu (眞人無夢). Sages Do, Not Dream. From the *Sayings of Zhuang Zhou (Chuang-Tzu)*.

Kohi Shihyo (光被四表). Spread Light in the Four Directions.

Shuitsu Muki (主一無適). Focus on the Goal.

Jiga Sakko (自我作古). Build on the Past to Make Your Present.

Jikyo Fusoku (自疆不息). Never Say Never.

Sanko Suicho (山高水長). Mountains Are High, Rivers Are Long. (Good deeds travel far—to the mountain peaks and along distant rivers.)

Waraku Zesho (和楽之処). Harmony Is a Blissful Place.

Suiteki Sekisen (水滴石穿). Drops of Water Wear Down a Stone.

Ryuryoku Kako (柳緑花紅). Willows Are Green, Flowers Are Red. This is a common Zen phrase, meaning, essentially, that things are just as they are.

Mushi Muhen (無私無偏). No Self, No Limit.

Meikyo Shisui (明鏡止水). Clear Mirror, Still Water. (The ideal state of mind is like a clear mirror and still water, polished and serene.)

Zenyu Shadeki (善遊者溺). Try to Float through Life and You Will End Up Sinking.

Yose Shii (与世推移). Life Is Change.

Kaibutsu Seimu (開物成務). Open Your Mind, Finish What You Start.

Hyakuda Fubatsu (百打不抜). One Hundred Blows, Not a Single Retreat.

Seinen Fujurai (盛年不重来). The Fullness of Youth Will Never Come Again. A verse by the Chinese poet Tao Yuanming (365–427). The second half of the couplet is *Ichijitsu Nansaishine* (一日難再晨), Each Day Passes on to the Next.

Riso Kenpyoshi (履霜堅氷到). When Frost Comes, Ice Will Form. The first sign of frost means that winter ice will eventually follow. Learn to recognize small signs before they become big events.

Oseki Jichokujin (枉尺而直尋). Prune the Small, Cultivate the Big.

Kikusui Getsu Zaite (掬水月在手). Scoop up Water, and the Moon Is Reflected in Your Hands. Another well-known Zen verse. The second half of the couplet is *Roka Ko Man'i* (弄花香萬衣), Hold Flowers and They Perfume Your Robe.

Rinshin Sokuchoro (林深則鳥楼). Deep in the Forest, Birds Perch.

The second half of the couplet is *Suiko Sakugyoyu* (水広則魚遊), In the Vast Ocean, Fish Swim. Think of your world as a large forest or deep ocean, not a confined, limiting space.

Kayoku Sokuhoshin (寡欲則保身). Few Desires Is the Best Shield.

Ryuryu Kaishinku (粒々皆辛苦). Each Grain of Rice Is Precious. The hard work a farmer puts in to nourish rice grains produces the food that sustains the world. We should work just as hard to cultivate our own body and mind.

Dozaiji Jikyoshoen (道在邇而諸求遠). The Way Is Near, but People Seek It Far Away. A phrase by the ancient Chinese philosopher Mengzi (fourth century B.C.E.).

Ryokin Sokijiro (良禽相木而楼). Clever Birds Know Exactly Where to Roost.

Goshin Hiseki Fukasen (吾心匪石不可転). One's Heart Is Not an Immovable Stone.

Shakuyushotan Sunyushocho (尺有所短 寸有所長). Long Has Short, Short Has Long.

Hosomachu Fufujijaku (蓬生麻中 不扶而直). Plants Planted Well Grow Straight.

Ryusuifufu Tosufuto (流水不腐 戸枢不蠹). Flowing Water Does Not Stagnate, Hardwood Is Not Bug Eaten.

Shunran Shuki Gufukahaiya (春蘭秋菊供不可廃也). Spring Orchids, Autumn Chrysanthemums, Both Are Delightful.

Shosofudoryoku Rodaijuyuhi (少壮不努力 老大徒優悲). No Effort in Youth, No Gain When Old.

The teachings of Kano are direct, clearly defined, and simple. They are based on the samurai virtues: proper demeanor, nonextravagance, no complaining about one's lot, loyalty, sincerity, fairness, forbearance, courage, self-reliance, and broad knowledge of the literary, fine, and martial arts. His teachings are easy to understand, but the challenge, our lifelong struggle, is to put those principles into practice.

精力善用自他共栄

Focused Effort, Maximum Effect, Mutual Wellbeing and Benefit.
—Kiissai

勝 制 道 順

Following the Way Produces Victory.
　—Konan

Jundo Seisho was one of Kano's favorite themes for calligraphy. As is often the case, the calligraphy lacks seals. Kano traveled widely, and at nearly every place he went people requested pieces of his calligraphy. Kano rarely carried his seals with him—he would have likely lost them because he was so absent-minded—so much calligraphy by Kano is not actually sealed.

道探

Search for the Way.
　—Kiissai

This was likely brushed near the end of Kano's life. The brushstrokes are supple and bright.

楽 是 勤

Movement Is Bliss.
　—Kɪɪssaɪ

力
必
達

Effort Ensures Results.
—KIISSAI

Another interpretation could be, "Strive and You Will Arrive." The first character is *chikara,* "strength." In judo, strength is not only physical but spiritual. In fact, without moral and spiritual strength even the most powerful force will eventually dissipate. Kano equated strength with ceaseless effort. If you make great effort, it will surely lead to great results regardless of the endeavor, regardless of the challenges. The brushwork is clear, lucid, and perfectly centered and balanced.

盡己竢成

Great Effort, Great Results.
—KONAN

The first characters are literally "Exhaust Oneself." The true road to success is effort, not natural talent or good luck.

丹
心
照
萬
古

A True Heart Shines Forever.
—KIISSAI

The first two characters are *tanshin*. Tan is the tan in *tanden*, the physical and spiritual center of a human being, believed to be located about two inches beneath the navel. Shin is "heart." *Tanshin* is a heart that is true, centered, and pure. The middle character is *terasu*, "shine." *Banko,* the last characters, mean "from the timeless past to the endless future." A heart that is true, determined, and sincere enables one to do great things, things that will never be forgotten. The brushstrokes are bold and well centered. Sumiyuki Kotani was once assisting Kano during a calligraphy session, grinding ink, preparing the paper, and drying the finished sheets. Kano was brushing one *Seiryoku Zenyo* after the other. He stopped and looked at Kotani. After thinking a bit, this is the saying he brushed for Kotani and gave to him.

抜 不 打 百

One Hundred Blows, Not a Single Retreat.
 —KONAN

This was the guiding principle of Kano's life.

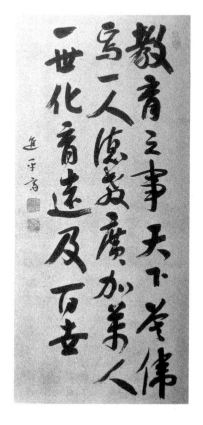

教育之事天下是偉
焉一人德教廣加萬人
一世化育遠及百世

Nothing under heaven is more important than education;
The teaching of one virtuous person can influence many;
That which has been learned well by one generation will pass on to a
  hundred.
  —SHINKOSAI

This calligraphy sums up Kano's philosophy of education.

無心而
入自然
之妙

之妙
入自然

無為而
窮変化
之神

窮変化
之神

With no mind, naturally enter marvelous activity;
With no effort, manifest unlimited magic movement.
—KAISHU KATSU YASUYOSHI

This calligraphy (now in very bad shape) was brushed on a huge signboard that was displayed for years at the Kodokan. No mind is *mushin* (無心) *Mushin* is the key to Zen and the martial arts. The state of no-mind is free of discriminating thoughts, judgments, analysis, or preconceptions. In such a state, one acts naturally, freely, marvelously. No effort is *mui* (無為) an expression favored by Taoists. One interpretation of *mui* could be "perfect equilibrium" between action and stillness, or in the case of judo, between the hard and the soft. Once that state of being is realized, action (technique) is executed effortlessly in unlimited variations. The character translated as magic is shin (神), which can also mean "divine," "deity," "essential," or "core."

The giant Kaishu Zen calligraphy displayed in the Kodokan. Kano sits facing his disciples at a kagami-baraki held at the Shimo-Tomisaka Dojo. The ecumenically minded Kaishu also brushed the Japanese translation of verse 18:12 from the Book of Proverbs ("Haughtiness goes before destruction; humility precedes honor") that hung on the wall of the Tenjo Christian Church in Okayama for years.

Resources

Primary Sources

The Collected Works of Kano Jigoro (嘉納治五郎大系), 15 vols., published under the direction of the Kodokan in 1988. The volumes most relevant to this biography are:

vol. 10, *Autobiography & Memoirs* (自伝回顧)
vol. 11, *The Biography of Kano Jigoro* (嘉納治五郎伝)
vol. 12, *Photo History* (写真集)
vol. 13, *Chronology* (年譜)

The material in the collected works is summarized in *The Collected Writings of Kano Jigoro* (嘉納治五郎著作集), 3 vols. (Gogatau Shobo, 1983).

Kano Jigoro (嘉納治五郎), also published under the direction of the Kodokan in 1964. Even though the book totals 770 pages, most of it concerns Kano's voluminous writings on education, philosophy, social issues, judo, general sports, the Olympic Games movement, and the like. Since Kano said the same things over and over (that's what teachers do), there is much repetition and the material itself is dated, albeit dated because many of Kano's ideas, progressive at the time, are now largely taken for granted.

Kano Jigoro: My Life and Judo (嘉納治五郎　私の生涯と柔道) (Nihon Tosho, 1997). One interesting thing: the chronology of Kano's life at the end includes Kano's salary for each post he assumed.

Kano Jigoro: Educator with Spirit and Action (嘉納治五郎—氣概と行動の教育者), ed. Committee for the Commemoration of the Birth of Jigoro Kano (University of Tsukuba, 2011). Since Tokyo Teacher Training College eventually became the University of Tsukuba, Kano is esteemed as the grand patriarch of the school. As the title implies, the book covers Kano's career as an educator, especially in physical education.

Kano Jigoro (嘉納治五郎), a biography by Zansei Koga (Dokosha, 1944).

Kano Jigoro (嘉納治五郎), by Nihei Kato (Shoyo Shoin, 1979).

Dainihon Judoshi (大日本柔道史; The Great History of Japanese Judo), by Sanzo Maruyama (Kodansha, 1939; rev. ed., Daiichi Shobo, 1984). Nearly 1,200 pages on the history of judo.

Works by Kano

Judo Primer (柔道教本上巻), vol. 1 (Sanseido, 1931). Written when Kano was seventy, this is a textbook for beginners in judo. One or two more volumes were planned but never completed.

There are four widely available books in English published under Kano's name:

Judo (Jujutsu), Japanese Tourist Library, vol. 16 (Maruzen, 1937).
Kodokan Judo (Kodansha USA, 1994).
Mind over Muscle: Writings from the Founder of Judo (Kodansha International, 2005).
Judo Memoirs of Jigoro Kano (Trafford Publishing, 2008).

"Jiujiutsu (柔術): The Old Samurai Art of Fighting without Weapons," by Rev. T. Lindsay and J. Kano, *Transactions of the Asiatic Society of Japan* 16. This paper was read on April 18, 1888. Most of the paper can be found on http://judoinfo.com, although the date the paper appeared is mistakenly given as 1887.

The Demonstration of Gentleness: Ju-no-Kata, demonstrated by Jigoro Kano, text by Trevor Leggett (W. Foulsham, 1964).

Several videos of Kano and Yamashita demonstrating koshiki-no-kata can be found on YouTube.

Secondary Sources

The June 1938 issue of the journal *Judo*, "In memoriam: Kano Jigoro Sensei," has many articles by his students and colleagues. In 1988, the Kodokan published a commemorative volume "On the 50th Anniversary of Kano Shihan's Death."

"Memories of My Father," by Noriko Watanuki, a one-page article in the journal *Kenkyu Kyoiku* 480 (June 1938): 20.

Secret Record of Japanese Judo (秘録日本柔道), by Raisuke Kudo (Nihon Sports Shinbunsha, 1975), has the best information about Kano and his top disciples.

The Men Who Made Judo (柔道を創った男たち), by Ichiyo Iizuka (Bungei Shunju, 1990), is also good.

Interesting Accounts of Japanese Martial Artists (日本格闘技おもしろ史話), by Kozo Kaku (Mainichi Shinbunsha, 1993), presents tales told about Kano and his disciples.

Hiden (秘伝) is a journal dedicated to the Japanese martial arts, past and present. Relevant articles from *Hiden* include:

"Early Days of the Kodokan" (July 2007): 14–26.

"Inagai Shinzo" (Oct. 1998): 46–51.

"Judo and the Martial Arts" (July 2004): 40–44.

"Judo Stories" (Mar. 1994): 106–11.

"Kano and the True Purpose of Kodokan Judo" (Jan. 1997): 80–85.

"Kano Jigoro" (Mar. 1995): 102–5.

"Kodokan: Itsutsu no Kata" (Oct. 10, 2007): 42–52.

"Mochizuki and Kano" (Nov. 1994): 50–52.

"Mochizuki and Kano" (Dec. 2003): 65–69.

"Saigo Shiro and Yama-arashi" (June 1997): 96–101.

"Secrets of Female Self-Defense," pt. 1 (Mar. 2004): 87–92.

"Secrets of Female Self-Defense," pt. 2 (Apr. 2004): 65–69.

"Secrets of Saigo Shiro," pt. 1 (May 1999): 117–22.

"Secrets of Saigo Shiro," pt. 2 (July 1999): 107–12.

"Tengu Nage" (May 1994): 102–7.

"Tomiki Kenji" (May 2007): 46–50.

"Yama-arashi" (July 1994): 97–101.

"Yokoyama Sakujiro," pt. 1 (Nov. 1993): 98–103.

"Yokoyama Sakujiro," pt. 2 (Jan. 1994): 105–10.

In English, there is *Jigoro Kano and the Kodokan*, ed. and trans. Alex Bennett (Kodokan, 2009), and *A History of Judo*, by Syd Hoare (Yanagi Books, 2009). Both are excellent, although more concerned with the history of judo rather than Kano's biography. The less said about Brian N. Watson's *The Father of Judo: A Biography of Jigoro Kano* (Kodansha International, 2000), the better. *Saving Japan's Martial Arts*, by Christopher M. Clarke (CreateSpace, 2011), is derived entirely from secondary sources and material available on the Internet and thus is not reliable. *Judo in the U.S.A.: A Century of Dedication*, by David Matsumoto (North Atlantic Books, 2005), is good on Kano and the early days of Kodokan judo in the United States. Matsumoto also compiled *An Introduction to Kodokan Judo: History and Philosophy* (Hon-no-Tomosha, 1996).

The Kano Society has three interesting articles on its website (www.kanosociety.org):

"Jigoro Kano in North America."

"Memories of Jigoro Kano's Visit to the London Budokwai in August 1933."

"The Death of Professor Jigoro Kano, Shihan."

The paper "Fulfilling His Duty as a Member: Jigoro Kano and the Japanese Bid for the 1940 Olympics," by Joseph R. Svinth, is available at http://ejmas.com.

There is a biography of Kano in French: *Jigoro Kano: Pere du Judo* (Budo, 2001).

The following relevant books in English have been written by Kano's direct students:

Judo: Japanese Physical Culture, by Sumitomo Arima (Mitsumura, 1908).

Judo, by Sakujiro Yokoyama and Eisuke Oshima (Nishodo, 1914).

Textbook of Judo (Jiu-Jitsu), vol. 1, by Dr. A. J. Ross (Official Handbook of the Australian Council of Judo, 1949).

Kodokan Judo, by Hikoichi Aida, trans. E. J. Harrison (Foulsham, 1956).

Canon of Judo: Principle and Technique, by Kyuzo Mifune (Seibundo-Shinkosha, 1958).

Judo and Aikido, by Kenji Tomiki, Japan Tourist Library, vol. 22 (Maruzen, 1967).

Kata of Kodokan Judo Revised, by Sumiyuki Osawa, Yoshimi Hirose, and Yuichi Kotani (Koyosan Bussan Kaisha, 1968).

Newaza of Judo, by Sumiyuki Osawa, Yoshimi Hirose, and Yuichi Kotani (Koyosan Bussan Kaisha, 1973).

Full-length biographies of Kano's Japanese students include the following.

Regarding Saigo Shiro: *Biography of Saigo Shiro* (史伝西郷四郎), by Noboru Makino (Shimazu Shobo, 1983); and *Yama-arashi: Saigo*

Shiro (山嵐—西郷四郎), ed. Gensaburo Akagi and Noboru Makino (Aizu Bukke-yashiki, 1987). Kurosawa's 1943 classic movie *Sugata Sanshiro* conveys the distinctive features of Saigo's life quite well. One interesting scene is a conversation between Sanshiro (Saigo) and Yano (Kano). Yano says, "Your technique may actually be better than mine, but judo is not about technique. Judo is to learn how to live so as to be a benefit to oneself and to society. You have a long way to go." As mentioned in the text, there has always been conjecture that, technically, Saigo was on a par with Kano, perhaps even better.

The Toughest Man Who Ever Lived: The History of Conde Koma, by Nori Bunasawa and John Murray (Kindle Edition, 2010).

One of a Kind—Toku Sanbo (柔道一代徳三宝), by Eizo Ibusuki (Nanpo Shimbun, 2007).

War Criminal: The Life and Death of Hirota Koki, by Saburo Shiroyama (Kodansha International, 1977). The title really means to say *"War Criminal?"* The subtitle of the original Japanese book is *The Man Who Devoted His Life to Preventing War Condemned to Death as a War Criminal. Rakujitsu Moyu* (落日燃), a full-length movie on Hirota (complete with a scene of him doing his "judo dance"), was produced in 2009. Hirota has become something of a hero among the Japanese. The book and movie depict well the tremendous social and political turmoil of the time and help us understand the difficult and complex challenges that Kano and Hirota had to face. Iris Chang's hysterical *Rape of Nanking* is a totally one-sided account of the tragedy that has unfortunately been taken as the gospel truth in many quarters. The Wikipedia article "Nanking Massacre Denial" actually presents all three sides of the story: Great Massacre School, Illusion School, and Middle of the Road School.

The Eighty-Three-Year-Old Lady Sanshiro That Soared So High (おんな三四郎83歳—宙をとぶ), by Yoko Naito (Efi Shuppan, 1996), is a biography of Katsuko Kosaki, the first female Kodokan black belt.

Bow from the Heart: The Life of Judo Master Keiko Fukuda, 9th Dan, by Patricia Harrington (Soko Joshi Judo Club, 2009).

This Is Kodokan Judo: The Story of 10th Dan Kotani Sumiyuki (これが 講道館柔道だ――名人小谷澄之十段の柔道一代), by Minoru Sugizaki (Ano hito sono hito Sha, 1988).

The complete story of the Santel affair can be found in *The First Battle of Kodokan Judo vs. Professional Wrestling* (講道館太プロレス 初対決), by Takeo Marushima (Shimazu Shobo, 2006).

Information on Kano's Chinese students is from widely scattered Japanese and Chinese sources, dictionaries, books, and the Internet. "The Man Who Molded Mao: Yang Changi and the First Generation of Chinese Communists," by Yeh Wen-hsin, *Modern China* 32 (Oct. 2006): 483–512, is informative. Another paper by Yeh Wen-hsin, "Historian and Courtesan: Chen Yinke and the Writing of Liu Rushi Biezhuan" (delivered as the Morrison Lecture, Australian National University, July 2003), is valuable as well. There is a 2011 documentary on Qiu Jin entitled *Autumn Gem* (available from autumn-gem. com). Jackie Chan starred as Huang Xing in the movie *1911*. The movie opens with a scene depicting the execution of Qiu Jin.

Bits and pieces on Kano's Caucasian students can be found here and there, mostly on the Internet. In addition to his classic *The Fighting Spirit of Japan* (Overlook Press, 1955), E. J. Harrison wrote a number of books on judo, all published originally by W. Foulsham:

Manual of Judo (1952).
Judo for Beginners (1953).
Judo on the Ground: (Katamewaza) The Oda 9th Dan Method (1954).
Judo for Women (1957).
Junior Judo (1957).
Judo: The Art of Jiujutsu (1960).
Judo for Young Girls (1961).

Information on Harrison himself can be found in two articles available at http://ejmas.com:

"A Résumé of My Chequered Career," by E. J. Harrison.
"Letters from E. J. Harrison to Robert W. Smith, 1950–1960," ed.
Joseph R. Svinth.

The interview with Moshe Feldenkrais in which he mentions his encounter with Kano can be found on the SemioPhysics website (http://semiophysics.com).

The article "Sarah Mayer: The First Non-Japanese Woman Awarded Black Belt in Judo" can be found on www.judoinfo.com.

For Katsu Kaishu, his complete works are available in Japanese: *Katsu Kaishu Zenshu* (勝海舟全集), 12 vols. (Keiso Shobo, 1997–98). There is an article on Kaishu by Romulus Hillsborough, "Katsu Kaishu: The Man Who Saved Early Modern Japan" (from *Tokyo Journal*, Summer 2002), at http://www.samurai-archives.com/kak.html. *Katz Awa: The Bismark of Japan* (with Kaishu's signature printed upside down on the cover), by the Christian minister E. Warren Clark (B. F. Buck & Company, 1904), is a tiny biography that praises Kaishu to the skies: "I owe him more gratitude and respect than to any individual I have ever met, and I have met great men in both heathen and Christian lands." Clark makes the dubious claim that Kaishu was a closet Christian, mostly because Kaishu behaved in such a charitable Christian manner and treated missionaries well (along with everyone else, Buddhist, Shintoist, or Confucian). While there isn't much else on Kaishu in English, the autobiography of his ne'er-do-well father, Kokichi, is available: *Misui's Story: The Autobiography of a Tokugawa Samurai*, trans. Teruko Craig (University of Arizona Press, 1988). Even though Kokichi was supposed to be a samurai, albeit of a low rank, he was more of a lowlife—beggar, thief, confidence man, thug, arms dealer, and other disreputable activities. Since his father was so dissolute, Kaishu had to take over as head of the Katsu family at age fifteen and try to settle his father's heavy debts. As is often the case, the son (Kaishu) turned out to be the complete opposite of the father (Kokichi).

For Tesshu Yamaoka, see *The Sword of No-Sword: Life of the Master Warrior Tesshu*, by John Stevens (Shambhala Publications, 1989). The book also contains a short chapter on Kaishu.

For Morihei Ueshiba, see *Invincible Warrior: A Pictorial Biography of Morihei Ueshiba*, by John Stevens (Shambhala Publications, 1999).

For Sokaku Takeda, see "Interview with Tokimune Takada," in *Daito-ryu Aikijujutsu: Conversations with Daito-ryu Masters*, ed. Stanley Pranin (Aiki News, 1996).

For Gishin Funakoshi, see *Three Budo Masters*, by John Stevens (Kodansha International, 1995). The three are Jigoro Kano, Gishin Funakoshi, and Morihei Ueshiba. The chapters on Funakoshi and Ueshiba are all right, but the one on Kano is not good and has been completely superseded by this biography.

For information on Fenollosa, Okakura, and Bigelow, see:

The Great Wave: Gilded Age Misfits, Japanese Eccentrics, and the Opening of Old Japan, by Christopher Benfey (Random House, 2003).
The Art of Scandal: The Life and Times of Isabella Stewart Gardner, by Douglass Shand-Tucci (HarperCollins, 1997), relates Gardner's love affair with Okakura and her connection to judo.
Okakura's *The Book of Tea*, the best edition of which is published by Benjamin Press, 2011. It has an excellent illustrated introduction on Okakura by Bruce Richardson.
Okakura Tenshin and the Museum of Fine Arts: Oct. 1999–March 2000 (Nagoya Boston Bijutsukan, 1999), a bilingual exhibition catalog, contains articles and illustrations of Okakura and Fenollosa.
Another Asia: Rabindranath Tagore and Okakura Tenshin, by Rustom Baraucha (Oxford University Press USA, 2009), discusses Okakura's books *The Ideals of the East* and *The Awakening of the East* in relation to Tagore's theories on the pan-Asian movement.

For Yanagi, see *The Unkown Craftsman: A Japanese Insight into Beauty* (Kodansha USA) and *In Pursuit of Composite Beauty: Yanagi Soetsu, His Aesthetics and Aspiration for Peace*, by Mari Nakami (Trans Pacific Press, 2011).

Photo Credits

The author and publisher gratefully acknowledge permission to reproduce copyright illustrations on the following pages:

From the Kodokan Archives: pp. 8, 18, 21, 26, 36, 45, 47, 50, 59, 60, 63, 64, 68, 74, 75, 76, 77, 154, 174, 204, 212, 213.
Courtesy of Bob Noha: pp. 15, 16.
Courtesy of Christine Kilian: p. 205.
Courtesy of Shozen Collection: p. 206.
Courtesy of Tusha Buntin: p. 207
Courtesy of Kaeru-an: p. 208
From private collections: pp. 49, 83, 117, 132, 135, 177, 203, 209, 210, 211.

Also Available from Shambhala Publications

Books by John Stevens

The Art of Peace

The real way of the warrior is based on compassion, wisdom, fearlessness, and love of nature. So taught the great Morihei Ueshiba (1883–1969), founder of the Japanese martial art of Aikido. Aikido is a discipline Ueshiba called the "Art of Peace." It offers a nonviolent way to victory in the face of conflict, and he believed that Aikido principles could be applied to all the challenges we face in life—in personal and business relationships, as well as in our interactions with society. These succinct and pithy teachings are drawn from his talks and writings.

Budo Secrets: Teachings of the Martial Arts Masters

In budo—which can be translated as "the way of brave and enlightened activity"—martial arts and spirituality merge at the highest level of skill. Budo Secrets contains the essential teachings of budo's greatest masters of Kendo, Karate, Judo, Aikido, and other disciplines. Timely and instructive, these writings are not just for martial artists—they're for anyone who wants to live life more courageously, with a greater sense of personal confidence and self-control, and with a deeper understanding of others. John Stevens has gathered an eclectic and historically rich collection of teachings that include principles and practice guidelines from training manuals and transmission scrolls, excerpts of texts on budo philosophy, and instructional tales gathered from a number of sources. Since many of the martial arts masters were also fine painters and calligraphers and used brush and ink as a teaching medium, Stevens has included their artwork throughout with explanation and commentary.

Dewdrops on a Lotus Leaf: Zen Poems of Ryokan

The Japanese poet-recluse Ryokan (1758–1831) is one of the most beloved figures of Asian literature, renowned for his beautiful verse, exquisite calligraphy, and eccentric character. Deceptively simple, Ryokan's poems transcend artifice, presenting spontaneous expressions of pure Zen spirit. Like his contemporary Thoreau, Ryokan celebrates nature and the natural life, but his poems touch the whole range of human experience: joy and sadness, pleasure and pain, enlightenment and illusion, love and loneliness. This collection of translations reflects the full spectrum of Ryokan's spiritual and poetic vision, including Japanese haiku, longer folk songs, and Chinese-style verse. Fifteen ink paintings by Koshi no Sengai (1895–1958) complement these translations and beautifully depict the spirit of this famous poet.

Invincible Warrior: A Pictorial Biography of Morihei Ueshiba, Founder of Aikido

This tells the fascinating story of the life of Morihei Ueshiba (1883–1969), whose quest for the true meaning of warriorship led to the creation of the martial art called Aikido, "The Art of Peace." Ueshiba—whose name means "abundant peace"—is considered by many to be one of the greatest martial artists who ever lived. His documented ability to disarm any attacker, throw a dozen men simultaneously, and down and pin opponents without touching them has accorded his life legendary status. John Stevens describes the people, events, and ideas that influenced Ueshiba's lifelong spiritual quest, which culminated in the development of unique teachings of Aikido. Illustrated with two hundred photographs of Ueshiba in action and filled with revealing anecdotes about his life and times, *Invincible Warrior* also offers valuable discussion of the Founder's conception of Aikido as a path of harmony and love, unifying body and mind, self and others, humans and the universe.

Lust for Enlightenment: Buddhism and Sex

Over the centuries, Buddhism has responded to sexuality in a variety of fascinating ways, sometimes, suppressing the sexual urge, sometimes sublimating it, sometimes cultivating it, and, on the highest levels, transforming it. This book reveals how Buddhists, beginning with Shakyamuni Buddha himself, relate to the "inner fire" that drives humankind. Included are chapters on the Buddha's love life before his enlightenment and his later relationships with women, the tantric approach to sex among Buddhists of ancient India, Tibet, China, and Japan; Zen in the art of love; and a positive discussion of women and Buddhism.

One Robe, One Bowl: The Zen Poetry of Ryokan

The hermit-monk Ryokan belongs in the tradition of the great Zen eccentrics of China and Japan. His poetry is that of the mature Zen master, its deceptive simplicity revealing an art that surpasses artifice. Although Ryokan was born in eighteenth-century Japan, his extraordinary poems, capturing in a few luminous phrases both the beauty and the pathos of human life, reach far beyond time and place to touch the springs of humanity.

The Shambhala Guide to Aikido

Aikido is the "Art of Peace," a discipline that emphasizes harmony and the peaceful resolution of conflict. Far more than a self-defense technique, Aikido is a physical and spiritual discipline that aims at unifying the body and spirit with the natural forces of the universe, fostering compassion, wisdom, and fearlessness. This Aikido handbook introduces the basic principles and practices of this popular martial art, including a biography of Morihei Ueshiba, the fundamental training methods and techniques with numerous photographs, philosophical and spiritual dimensions of Aikido, tips on how to choose an instructor, a glossary of important terms, and suggestions for further reading.

The Sword of No-Sword: Life of the Master Warrior Tesshu

Master swordsman, calligrapher, and Zen practitioner, Yamaoka Tesshu is a seminal figure in martial arts history. John Stevens's biography is a fascinating, detailed account of Tesshu's remarkable life. From Tesshu's superhuman feats of endurance and keen perception in life-threatening situations, to his skillful handling of military affairs during the politically volatile era of early nineteenth-century Japan, Stevens recounts the stories that have made Tesshu a legend.

Zen Bow, Zen Arrow: The Life and Teachings of Awa Kenzo, the Archery Master from Zen in the Art of Archery

Awa Kenzo (1880–1939), Zen and kyudo (archery) master, gained worldwide renown after the publication of Eugen Herrigel's cult classic Zen in the Art of Archery in 1953. In this collection of inspirational stories and teachings from Kenzo's life, we are taken to the very core of martial practice. Kenzo lived and taught at a pivotal time in Japan's history, when martial arts were practiced primarily for self-cultivation, and his wise and penetrating instructions for practice (and life)—including aphorisms, poetry, instructional lists, and calligraphy—are infused with the spirit of Zen. Kenzo uses the metaphor of the bow and arrow to challenge the practitioner to look deeply into his or her own true nature.